MATTHEW MANNING'S
GUIDE TO SELF-HEALING

A comprehensive and important new book which gives positive
advice to enable the reader to take responsibility for his or her
own health and well-being.

D1387329

MATTHEW MANNING'S GUIDE TO SELF-HEALING

THORSONS PUBLISHING GROUP

First published 1989

© Matthew Manning 1989

British Library Cataloguing in Publication Data

Manning, Matthew
Matthew Manning's guide to self-healing.
1. Mental healing
I. Title
615.8'51

ISBN 0-7225-1626-6

*Published by Thorsons Publishers Limited,
Wellingborough, Northamptonshire NN8 2RQ, England*

Printed in Great Britain by Billing & Sons Ltd, Worcester

Typeset by Harper Phototypesetters Limited, Northampton

1 3 5 7 9 10 8 6 4 2

Contents

Foreword

Matthew Manning is an extraordinary young man. There is no doubt about that. I believe the many people who have been helped by him could have written this foreword more astutely than I.

I have seen many patients who have previously attended Matthew for healing; every one of them, without exception, has gained considerably from their meeting with him. The confidence they have had in his work played a major role in their recovery and outlook on life.

Matthew's openness and willingness to learn, combined with the special natural powers he possesses, make him a unique person in an area surrounded by suspicion and mystique.

My many years training as a doctor, anaesthetist and hypnotherapist have taught me how much we do *not* know about the body and its healing processes. Matthew's powers are not discussed in medical textbooks, but I can verify their efficacy from those of his patients I have met.

The more we learn about ourselves and our self-healing potential, the less likely we are to require drugs or 'someone else to fix us' by injections, operations or the multitude of laboratory tests now 'routine' in the medical profession. I hope one day the work of healers like Matthew will be alongside the medical profession — acknowledged, understood and a part of the healing routine available to those in need.

I believe this book will play its part in allowing that enlightenment to take place and, in time, Matthew's work will be viewed in the perspective of the healing arts of which medicine is but one.

It is interesting that my pathway towards understanding health and illness came through being a general practitioner, then an anaesthetist and lastly using hypnotherapy and counselling to help people with their problems. Matthew's route was vastly different, yet we have so much in common with regard to our views of disease — its causation and maintenance — that one would think we attended the same schooling.

For the many people who will be unable to see Matthew personally, this book represents him and his views. The experience and case histories expressed within these pages will be very helpful in understanding ways and attitudes relating to your problems. Applying his directions to your own personal experiences will be a major factor in maintaining your health — either by the prevention or cure of illness.

He has written in a simple and easily-read way and the reference to case histories to illustrate his points makes it all the more authentic. Self-healing requires us to take responsibility for our health and make a commitment to carry out what is needed to maintain it. I believe this book will provide a solid basis from which to progress towards a healthier life.

DR BRIAN ROET
MB, BS, BA, FFA, RACS

1.

Why do we get ill?

I had been treating Mary, a young woman suffering from Hodgkin's disease (a form of cancer which affects the glandular system) for six months. When I first saw her the medical prognosis was not optimistic. Orthodox medical treatment was not inhibiting the progress of the disease. But now, she had received the news that her cancer was in remission.

The following week she had a nervous breakdown. At the time nobody could understand why Mary should feel so depressed at this point because suddenly the threat that had been hanging over her life was lifted.

'I'm frightened of life and of living,' she told me. 'In a way dying is easier than living.'

The simple fact was that her breakdown occurred because she couldn't cope with life. It has been said that for many people illness can be a socially acceptable form of suicide. This might seem an unlikely over-dramatization and, if it were so, would anyone read this book?

This is not necessarily a new idea. As far back as the second century AD Galen, the well-known Roman physician, observed that depressed women, not cheerful ones, tended to develop breast cancer. In the nineteenth century, Sir James Paget wrote that cases of deferred hope and of disappointment bring on the growth of cancer. In 1926 Elida Evans, a Jungian analyst, studied one hundred cancer patients and found that many had lost an important emotional relationship before the onset of the disease.

Another patient of mine was a girl called Monica. She was twenty-seven years old and was suffering from advanced multiple sclerosis (MS) which left her in a wheel-chair with little movement, 10 percent vision and incontinence. She was as disabled mentally, emotionally and spiritually as she was physically. Normally when I begin to treat a new patient I will first spend some time talking to them about the history of their problem and what they can do to combat it. With Monica I felt it best to start my healing treatment without any preliminary conversation. I always use music whilst I am treating patients, and midway through the session I felt her legs moving. Opening my eyes I saw that she was holding her arms crossed against her body, that she had thrown her head back and appeared to be about to scream. Instead she burst into tears. After a little while she became very self-conscious, as she was obviously aware that I was watching her behaviour, and she made an effort to pull herself together. Later she told me that she had always been told that crying was a sign of weakness. When the session had finished she left the Centre and I still had not really discovered much about her. The following day she returned for a second consultation, and once more I felt it best at this point not to say too much. Again, halfway through the session, she reacted by holding herself tightly and crying almost uncontrollably. When I had finished we sat and talked for some time. I asked her to tell me about any possible emotional trauma or loss that she might have experienced perhaps six months to two years prior to the onset of the disease. The story that emerged was fascinating.

When Monica was a teenager she met a young man and they started to date regularly. After a couple of years they became engaged and planned to marry when she was eighteen. Everything was arranged and the wedding date was fixed. Eight weeks before the marriage was due to take place her fiancé walked out on her and the wedding was cancelled. She was completely devastated. She had never had a relationship with anybody else and she could not bear to live without him. She locked herself into her parent's bathroom and slashed her wrists with one of her father's razor blades. She now showed me the scars, and they were clearly not like the series of small nicks that one sees with somebody who is making a 'suicide' attempt in order to draw attention to themselves. She had evidently meant to kill herself. However, her parents realized what had happened, broke down the bathroom door, and rushed her to hospital where she was saved from bleeding to death. Six months later she developed the first symptoms of MS: tingling in the hands and legs, blurred vision and partial loss of vision. She had actually tried to commit suicide but had been thwarted. Her illness had the potential to do the same thing, but it is much more difficult for others to prevent. However, although diagnosed as suffering from MS she was still able to work and could walk with the aid of a stick. Six years later she married someone else. Tragically, after ten months the marriage collapsed as her husband could not cope with a disabled wife. Within weeks she had deteriorated rapidly to the state she was in when she came to see me.

Those who attempt suicide rarely intend to succeed and almost always hope to be found by someone else before it goes too far. One often hears of distraught people who have threatened to jump from high buildings or bridges, only to be talked out of it by a police officer. If they really wanted to jump they would do so, but instead they stand and shout to draw attention to themselves. Those who make an attempt on their lives usually do so because they have unresolved problems that have piled up against them in an apparently insoluble way. There is something wrong in their lives which needs to be confronted in order to find a practical solution. That is also the way in which I view much illness. I really do not accept that people intend to kill themselves through disease but rather that the disease is a sign that there is something wrong in their lives. This also represents the greatest gulf between orthodox Western medicine and many of the complementary therapies such as my own. Orthodox methods seek to heal symptoms by drugs or surgery, but they tend to ignore the cause. Unless one treats the cause, the chances are great that the problem will recur again at some future time.

My approach relies on reversing negative psychological and emotional trends, encouraging the patient not to feel trapped and victimized by life and to deal with problems in a more positive, creative way. For example, I use goal-setting to help re-establish a connection with life. This represents a recommitment to life, and the body's defences respond to new feelings of hope by taking up the fight against illness. Some people, though, would rather die than recommit themselves to life.

Why should some people find death preferable to life? Often it is because they have never discovered their own identity or lived their own life. Therefore, they have died to their own authentic existence for years. These 'little daily deaths' can eventually bring about a state of hopelessness that expresses itself in a life-threatening illness. Hopelessness will often stem from the lifetime habit of pleasing others, rather than living one's authentic life. When pleasing others becomes such a burden, and so far from what one really wanted to do in life, death becomes preferable.

I have found that there are almost as many different reasons for people developing illness as people themselves. There are some illness-triggering mechanisms which seem more prevalent than others and interestingly many of these seem to stem from childhood. For example, children will often learn that if they have a test at school for which they have not done their homework there is a very simple way out of it. They tell their mother that they have a sore throat and they are then kept at home for the day. The patterning has been learned and stored from an early age. If later in life that same person is involved in a boring or unsatisfactory job, illness may well be a legitimate escape route.

Maybe when you were a child a younger brother or sister appeared on the scene and you believed that your parents' love and attention had been switched to this younger sibling. But when you were ill in bed with measles, your mother suddenly seemed to give you much more love and care. You learn that there is a connection then between being ill and gaining sympathy or love.

Is your illness perhaps a means of getting out of a job or a situation that you cannot avoid in any other way? Does it shift the balance in a relationship by altering someone else's attitude or behaviour towards you? Does it perhaps strengthen a relationship?

One of the initial questions I ask patients at the Centre is about their state of employment, because whether they are employed, self-employed, retired or unemployed also appears to have a bearing upon health. Over 80 percent of my patients are either working for somebody else or unemployed; self-employed patients are in the minority. In September 1977, Which? magazine published a survey of 24,000 of its readers to find out what kind of job gave the greatest job satisfaction. Those who were most satisfied were usually working for a small firm, where they had a responsible position, had a heavy work load, worked long hours but had some control over what they did. They also felt their work was important and tended to be better paid than average. The results of Which?'s survey 'How you rate your jobs' is shown opposite.

Which? found that the majority of the jobs high on the job satisfaction list were those where people had a higher than average degree of control over how they did the job, and that many of them were in professional and vocational jobs. If we feel that we are doing something important in our job we gain satisfaction. A craftsman is more likely to be happy in his work than a man who works on an assembly line and never sees the end product of his efforts. We all need to feel that what we do is important, and this is one of the greatest sources of stress for many people. Some of the men that I treat for stress-related problems have trouble in expressing themselves because they have never had the opportunity to do so during their working lives. One London hospital now runs dancing classes for men being treated in the coronary care unit so that they have an opportunity to express themselves more fully.

In Sweden a survey of workers taking tranquillizers for stress-related problems found that those who took most pills were those who had least control over their jobs. The workers who needed few if any drugs were gardeners or university researchers — people not caught up in a fast pace of life. A more recent survey of drivers of single-manned

Overall, how satisfied are you with your present job?

More than averagely satisfied	% very satisfied	Less than averagely satisfied	% very satisfied
clergyman	58	economist	19
company director	48	computer programmer/ systems analyst	18
farmer/horticulturalist	48		
optician	45	laboratory assistant	18
solicitor/barrister	43	skilled manual jobs (e.g. engineer, printer, welder)	18
primary school teacher	42		
shopkeeper	42		
university/polytechnic teacher	41	engineer (all professional types, including civil, electrical, electronic and mechanical)	17
photographer/ cameraman	39		
insurance broker	37	secretarial and clerical jobs (e.g. secretary, typist, telephonist)	17
vet	37		
actor/musician	36	management trainee	16
social worker/probation officer	35	unskilled manual jobs (e.g. building labourer, shop assistant)	15
		market researcher	14
		research officer/assistant	14
		actuary	11
		draughtsmen	8

buses in London found that they were more prone to illness and anxiety than double crews. The survey by Dr Michael Joffe of the London Hospital Medical College says there is a disturbing level of health problems among drivers who also collect fares.

In the book *How to survive the 9–5*, Martin Lucas lists fifteen of the most important sources of satisfaction or dissatisfaction which people describe at work. Answer yes or no for each item according to how you feel about that particular aspect of your job. Are you satisfied with:

● The physical work conditions?
● Your colleagues?
● Your salary?
● Industrial relations between management and staff?
● Your hours of work?
● The freedom to choose your own method of working?
● The recognition you get for good work?

- Your immediate boss?
- The way you are managed?
- The attention paid to suggestions you make?
- The amount of responsibility you are given?
- The opportunity to use your abilities?
- The amount of variety in your job?
- Your chance of promotion?
- Your job security?

People who are self-employed probably feel that they have much greater control of their lives. For the person employed by a large company with little or no job satisfaction and no feeling of involvement in an end product, illness may be an efficient means of asserting control over events. It could also be argued that the self-employed person is better at solving problems within relationships than the person who is employed.

Both unemployment and retirement can bring problems too because being out of work can cause more problems than little or no job satisfaction. A recent study by Dr Norman Beale showed that redundancy or the threat of it resulted in a 20 percent increase in the number of consultations with GPs by workers and their families, and a 60 percent rise in hospital visits. He found an 11 percent increase in illness when jobs were insecure or lost compared with a 9 percent decrease among workers in other local firms who had secure jobs. 'The results suggest that the threat of redundancy is a stress which is equal to, if not greater than, the actual event', wrote Dr Beale in the *Journal of the Royal College of General Practitioners*.

For the unemployed there are undoubtedly feelings of depression and lack of self-worth which can have a detrimental effect on the body. Curiously most people do not anticipate retirement as a stressful period of their lives as it has always been portrayed as the time when one can do all the things that one did not have time for whilst working. Yet my observations are that this major change in life style can frequently precipitate major illness. Indeed, statistics suggest that Mr Average in Britain dies within six months of retirement.

The greatest lesson we can learn from these observations is one of attitude. When the Corby Steelworks were closed down some years ago, it was noted that within a year the incidence of illness (and especially that which was stress related) had increased quite significantly. Since that time numerous reports have been published to link unemployment with sickness. But there is a striking and apparently inexplicable anomaly. The acting profession has the highest rate of unemployment at around 70 percent and yet maintains the lowest incidence of illness. An out of work actor never says that he is redundant but rather that he is resting. Here there is a world of difference between the two messages that he could give himself. The power of self-instruction or, as I prefer to call it, affirmation, is enormous. These affirmations form a major part of all the self-help cassettes that I produce.

I have always felt that the world comprises basically two types of people: those who worry and those who don't! The worrier is the person who rolls out of bed in the morning saying 'Oh God! Not another day. What will go wrong today?' They always feel that they won't succeed, they invariably imagine the worst, and they usually expect to be let down. The non-worrier, however, will jump out of bed in the morning, pull open the curtains, and declare that it is going to be a wonderful day. For those people things never seem to go wrong, everything works out, they are great at problem solving, and they always land on their feet. It is all to do with how you see yourself and the affirmations that you programme into the system.

How often have you heard friends or people in the street using affirmations quite unwittingly? There is the person who describes their job as a real pain in the neck and then later wonders why their neck feels so tense or why they have to endure worn discs in the neck. There is the person who describes their errant teenage daughter as a real headache, never appreciating why they seem to get a migraine when she is around. Have you heard the person who tells you that something gets on their nerves; you then watch their hands shaking as they put sugar in their tea? If I restricted myself to these familiar examples you would be forgiven for thinking that I was being flippant. However, I believe that language reveals more of the mind–body links than may have been previously acknowledged.

I once treated a lady who had been embroiled in a family row that had left her filled with anger. Six weeks later, she explained to me, she had developed raging conjunctivitis. She had been quite unaware of the descriptive language she had used but I had immediately noted her use of the word 'rage'. The doctor had prescribed some antibiotics which had cleared up the conjunctivitis but had done nothing for the rage. Six months later she developed a malignant breast tumour.

Another young woman had been partner to a very turbulent marriage which had eventually ended in an acrimonious divorce. She told me that she could remember shouting at her husband to stop arguing because it made her sick. 'You make me sick to the stomach,' she reported having shouted at him on several occasions. She developed stomach cancer a year after the marriage broke up.

These are all examples of what I call the negative affirmation. If we can be so adept at this, why can we not learn to use positive affirmations in order to help promote good health? One could dismiss the above examples as amusing coincidences were it not for the fact that they appear with alarming regularity in my patients' initial written reports and in their subsequent conversation. Additionally a recently published medical report seems to support my idea.

Wouter Oosterhuis, a doctor working at the University at Amsterdam, investigated the cases of 500 people, both men and women, who had complained of pain for which no physical cause could be found. He asked them about problems at home and at work during the time they experienced the pain. Of 331 who suffered from feelings of aggression, 329 suffered pains in the neck. Of those who experienced fear nine out of ten complained of a pain in the abdomen. And of those who complained of despair, six out of ten suffered from pain in the lower back, just above the seat. His findings showed that these different emotions affect quite different parts of our body.

Oosterhuis says that it is important to recognize these patients so that they can be given psychological support or be guided into solving the practical problems that trouble them. If the emotional cause of the pain is not recognized and they are treated as if for a physical pain, there is a danger of them becoming chronic patients with intractable pain. So those old and rather crude sayings such as 'a pain in the backside' may well have medical significance!

The point is that positive affirmations do achieve results. They break the circuit of negative thinking that so often the patient has acquired; they help to call a halt to the production of stress hormones caused by anxiety, and the more you use them the more you actually *become* like the person for whom you are now affirming. Most importantly affirmations can help you to release feelings of guilt, anger or even grief from past events that may have helped contribute to your illness. As I frequently tell people: you cannot change past events but you do have a choice as to how you see them.

It is very clear from my records that certain emotional responses to life crises or difficulties do seem to prompt particular types of illness. I know that many doctors are sceptical of this and will argue that there is no evidence to support such a claim. However, there is again medical evidence to reinforce this idea.

In 1981 a team of researchers at London's Westminster Hospital discovered that people with rheumatoid arthritis had suffered their first attack of the disease not long after a major upset in their life, such as bereavement, divorce or job loss. Like other doctors who have looked for a possible psychosomatic factor in rheumatoid arthritis, they also found that patients often came from families where the mother was a tyrannical figure, hard to love but difficult to break away from.

The evidence to link emotional stress with heart disease is much stornger. A study was carried out by two American cardiologists, Meyer Friedman and Ray Roseman, who studied a group of accountants over a six-month period. They were asked to keep a meticulous record of what they ate in order to determine whether a food factor affected their hearts. As April, the busiest time of the year for accountants, approached, their cholesterol levels rose sharply even though their diets had not changed. Once the April deadline for tax returns had passed and their work-load was reduced, their cholesterol levels dropped too.

From an early stage it was apparent to me that there was a link between the loss of a stabilizing influence in life and the subsequent diagnosis of cancer. Some years ago I treated a middle-aged lady who had, two years before her cancer was discovered, been divorced. She had only one child, a teenaged daughter with whom she lived and around whom her life revolved. She came for healing with cancer of the spine. She was unable to drive herself, was in considerable pain and could only just walk with the aid of crutches. Over the next three months she progressed well and was able to stop taking pain-killers. She gained strength and was able to walk unaided and to drive her car short distances.

One night the daughter and her boyfriend were killed in a car crash. Within six weeks my patient, who had been doing so well, had relapsed and died. It seemed to me that the cancer had been precipitated by the loss of her husband. She had then transferred all her attentions to her only daughter who may well have been a contributing factor to the short period of recovery she experienced. When her daughter died she obviously had little left to live for.

A high proportion of my adult cancer patients display a common pattern of having lost a stabilizing influence in their life six to eighteen months before their disease was first noticed or diagnosed. This stabilizing influence is generally a spouse who may be lost due to death, divorce or separation; it can be the loss of a job; or, in some cases, it may be a change in geographic locality, where typically a husband's job is changed to another area of the country and the wife feels a loss of roots or close friends.

I must emphasize one point, however. I am not claiming that each person who experiences a loss is going to develop cancer. Rather, it is your *response* to that loss which appears to be the decisive factor. A middle-aged man who has held a responsible job with one company for over twenty years and who is then made redundant has two choices as to his response. He can tell himself that his life is finished, that there is nothing for him to do and that he is redundant. My records show that he is more likely to come to the Centre with a major health problem than the same man who responds to that situation by telling himself that his job loss now provides the perfect opportunity to do all those things in life that he had always wanted to do. He can now start his own business, build the house that he has never had time to even start on previously, or travel to all the places he was always too busy to visit before. Again, it is ultimately a question of the messages about the loss that you give yourself. The person who is most vulnerable will respond to the loss situation with a reaction of total helplessness and hopelessness and feel that events are quite outside their control.

I have observed other patterns with different illnesses. A common one is a link with anger, often suppressed, and multiple allergies. One of my patients, when questioned about any experiences prior to the onset of her allergic reactions, was quite unable to make any such association. I explained that this need not apply to every patient and maybe she was an exception. Some weeks later I was presenting a seminar on self-healing in London and the same lady was in the audience. I began to share my views on the anger and allergy link when she stood up and vociferously berated me for still saying the same thing! 'You told me that last month,' she exclaimed, 'and even though I told you it was wrong, you are still saying it.' The audience broke into laughter which merely served to heighten her demonstrated anger. Clearly she was either unaware of her anger or unwilling to confront it. Needless to say, she never came back.

I was told another story by a lady who had overcome her allergies using one of my cassettes. Suffering from multiple allergies she had bought my cassette, *Resisting Allergies*, after a lecture I had given. Only months later did she actually listen to it. Whilst listening to the relaxation and self-healing exercise included on it she had a most unusual experience. Suddenly a long-suppressed memory of an incident with her step-father some twenty years earlier had surfaced. It was something that she had not given any thought to in years but suddenly she found herself filled with raw rage. I don't know what the incident was but she told me that she had been unable to tell anybody about it all these years for fear of hurting her mother. The tape though had brought it all back. For a week she punched pillows and cushions and cried and screamed until it seemed that her anger, like a storm, had vented itself. From that time on she has been able to eat all the foods which previously had caused her such violent reactions.

Some of my arthritic patients, especially those with rheumatoid arthritis, have a common experience which is similar to that discovered by the Westminster Hospital researchers. Often they have been involved in a relationship with a strong and domineering partner. There have been many things in life that they have at various times wanted to do but they have always felt held back by their partner's life style or progress. Somehow, symbolically, the arthritis, which stiffens their joints and restricts their movement, prevents them from moving towards those things they had always wanted to do for themselves. Rather than blame their partner for inhibiting them in their own pursuits, they are able to blame the illness.

Over-strong partners also appear to have a bearing on another serious problem that I have treated on numerous occasions: Parkinson's disease. Here it seems that there is often a strong feeling of fear that has acted as a precipitating factor. For example, I have worked with a number of women who have been married to a strong partner who has perhaps done too much for them. He may have over-protected her from the outside world. When he suddenly and unexpectedly dies she is filled with fears about how she will cope. It is not perhaps socially acceptable to shake because you are fearful in this situation but it is socially acceptable if you suffer a disease which causes a similar physical response. I remember a gentleman with Parkinson's disease who came to a seminar of mine. Afterwards he approached me and I thought he was going to criticize me for the comments I had made about the illness afflicting him. On the contrary, he told me that it had been worth his while to come to the seminar just to hear my comments about Parkinson's disease. During the last war he had flown thirty-three bombing missions over Germany and each time he set off he was terrified that he would be shot down never to return. He could not show his feelings of fear to the rest of his bomber crew and so he learned to suppress them and maintain a typically English stiff upper lip. A couple of years after being discharged from the RAF after the war he developed a slight tremor, and it was only years later as his shaking worsened that his disease was diagnosed.

Even a problem as simple as a bad back often has an underlying triggering factor. Frequently the back-pain sufferer is the person who carries the weight of the world on their shoulders. Like the legendary Hercules they begin to bend and stoop under the weight until finally their back gives way.

It may be that you really cannot find any specific trigger mechanism for your illness, or it may be that you have a recurring problem. If this is the case it is worth considering what gains you may be achieving by maintaining the problem.

We all know that if we deprive ourselves of food and water for a sufficient number of days we can drastically damage our health and eventually die. Yet we seem blind to the equal danger of an emotional hunger strike. Throughout our life we receive strokes from everybody around us. A stroke is a form of recognition or stimulation which arouses feelings. There are two kinds of stroke: positive and negative. A positive stroke is a compliment from someone, a kind word, or a smile. A negative stroke would be someone else's hurtful words, a cold stare, or a reprimand. In reality, whether people are unpleasant or charming toward you, you are being stroked. It is confirmation that we exist and is essential for our survival. If we are not successful in getting our needs met in positive, life-affirming ways, we will look for them in negative, death-promoting ways rather than suffer being ignored. The football hooligan, for example, gets short-term attention from the police, his parents, the courts and the media. He is getting strokes, and even if they are negative it is preferable to going through life unnoticed. That would be worse than the punishment of his destructive behaviour.

I also find that with my cancer patients the loss of their stabilizing influence also constitutes a loss of their source of positive strokes. Men may acquire their strokes from their career or their wife; women may acquire theirs from their family or community. When the source of positive strokes is lost it can lead to destructive means of compensation. Nobody wants to be ill but we all need our strokes. Unfortunately, as I frequently observe, people sometimes get strokes for the first time from their family when they are ill. They then hold on to the illness to maintain the strokes.

Strokes also create feelings and emotions within us. If someone pays you an unexpected compliment it will leave you happy and cheerful for the rest of the day. If someone puts you down it can depress you for hours. Because of the way we are brought up as children these emotional responses tend to get classified as 'good' or 'bad'. For example, smiling passive behaviour is rewarded in children whereas displays of fear, anger or sadness are often punished. This leads to a suppression or dulling of our emotions in general. We lose trust in our own experience. I believe it is this running away from or burying our emotions that leads to disease in later life.

It is my goal to show people that we are all special in our own way. I hope to highlight the effect of attitudes and therefore the importance of positive attitudes towards a greater quality of living. I want my patients to enjoy life, to realize their potential and to realize that they have choices.

You have the ability to choose a more positive alternative instead of self-destructive attitudes. Learn not to project your past experiences of pain into the future or you will spend the rest of your life haunted with fear. Fear of emotions, mistakes, success, failure, other people, yourself, weakness or rejection. There is only one time that is important and that is now. You can spend the rest of life looking backwards or worrying about the future and miss the present. You may not be able to change past events but you can change your thoughts, emotions and attitudes towards them. That for me is where true healing begins.

This is called attitudinal healing. This is healing of the mind, correcting our misperceptions and changing how we perceive the world, others, and ourselves. It allows one to heal one's relationships, to heal negative, fearful thoughts, and to experience inner peace, well being, love and health.

Attitudinal healing's founder, and now consultant, is Dr Gerald Jampolsky, a psychiatrist who has worked mainly with children who have cancer, and has achieved remarkable results with alternative healing methods. It was while Jampolsky was working as a student doctor in Boston in 1949 that he first became interested in cancer, and the 'will to live' and the 'will to die', and learnt that through hypnotic suggestion a wart could be made to disappear. It was on this basis that he realized that through mental imagery and suggestion one could rid themselves of pain and change their perception and illusion of illness. That, in fact, there was *nothing* the mind could *not* do.

When we think someone is angry or is attacking us we choose, in attitudinal healing, to see that person not as attacking us, but just as being scared. We learn that in extending our love to others and helping others with no expectation of anything in return, we also help ourselves. As we focus on others' fears and problems, our own seem to dissolve and peace of mind prevails.

There are ten areas where you are most likely to encounter negativity entering your life. By observing and changing these negative areas into *positive* areas, you can instigate new perspectives in situations that will ultimately benefit your health and happiness. The following points will help you in this way:

1. Think well of yourself and your accomplishments and take opportunity to re-affirm these regularly. (The basis to being able to love or respect anyone else is to first learn to love and value your own self.)
2. Rather than worry or complain about what you do not have, appreciate what you do have. (Remember, we get what we need in life, not always what we want.)

3. Surround yourself with beauty and light, inwardly and outwardly. (Your environment is external but your spirit is internal and eternal.)

4. Do not allow another's criticism to affect you. Have faith in yourself and your ability. (Remember, criticism is also another way of expressing jealousy and often appears in those who lack confidence and self-worth; the unhappy, troubled person can also be critical.)

5. Accept each new circumstance as an opportunity for growth and self-improvement. (We learn from experience, whether good or bad.)

6. Remember: Every cloud has a silver lining. Even negative life events have a reason for happening. (All events in life come as part of the learning process.)

7. Leave yesterday's sadness behind you and look forward to tomorrow with hope and joy. (Why worry over a past event that you have no means in the present of changing? Let it go.)

8. We all make mistakes. Don't fret over what is too late to change. Store it in your bank of experience. (Yesterday's mistake can be tomorrow's triumph.)

9. Though you may still *want* it, let go that which you no longer *need*. (Let the outworn go so that you can be open and receptive to new circumstances.)

10. We all shelter under the same umbrella of a universal Consciousness ('When to the new eyes of thee/All things by immortal power,/Near or far,/Hiddenly/To each other linkèd are,/That thou canst not stir a flower/Without troubling of a star.' Francis Thompson.)

Learn that you are free. Free to question, feel, think, choose, communicate, change, assert, accept, forgive, release, know, be, live and love.

I cannot change you. You decide on, and are responsible for, the necessary changes in your life. I do not compete with anybody else and I do not offer a substitute for any other therapies or medical care you may be receiving. I hope to inspire you to laugh, smile and realize your potential.

2.

Stress: it's a killer

Stress now accounts for more lost working days in the United Kingdom than strikes. Its effect upon our health is quite catastrophic yet most of us choose to do nothing about it even though preventative action is so simple. It is the most common component in the illness of virtually all the people who seek my help.

We are all under some form of stress or strain — I don't believe it's possible to live without it. The only person without stress is a dead one! But gradation occurs between creative and constructive stress and a destructive or immobilizing stress. The use of the word stress, as applied to human beings, was started in the 1930s by a Canadian physiologist, Professor Hans Selye. Before that it was a word generally used by engineers constructing bridges. Selye was involved in a research programme to study the hormonal functions of rats. During his experiments he would inject the animals with various toxic or impure substances and after their demise would dissect them to discover what physical changes had occurred. Regardless of what the rats had been injected with, Selye found that their tissue almost always showed the same signs of damage. Their lymph nodes, which help to rid the body of outside invaders such as infection or virus, had become wasted and they suffered from ulcers in their digestive tracts and were very thin. Later he found that there were three basic stages of response to any prolonged negative stimuli. What happened to Selye's rats can also happen to us.

First there was an alarm reaction during which the body mobilized the necessary resources to deal with the perceived threat or attack. He discovered that the adrenal glands which manufacture hormones to combat disease came under heavy pressure at this time. The second phase occurred when the rat learned, apparently, to cope with the negative stimulus and its glands would produce sufficient hormones for it to recover. This 'adaption period', as Selye called it, did not last forever; if the stimulus was maintained the rat went into a sudden decline and died.

The human nervous system is designed in just the same way as that of animals and it has two branches. There is the sympathetic, which responds to an outer stimulus by producing the hormones we need to take action, and the parasympathetic, which is responsible for rest, digestion and restoring the hormone content of the body to a balanced state. What humans tend to do is to undergo a stimulus or stress which produces the hormones required for action but don't or can't follow this up with action or the necessary recuperation period. Think how animals behave in the wild: they get hungry, they hunt, they eat, and then they sleep. Professor Selye concluded that there were two forms of stress. There is what he called 'eustress', which is the stress of winning or achievement, and this brings about positive feelings. 'Distress', on the other hand, is the stress of losing, when we feel inadequate, insecure, helpless, despairing and disappointed. Usually when we refer to stress we actually mean Selye's distress. However, when stress is properly handled it provides the motivation to overcome the obstacles preventing us from reaching our hopes and goals — this is eustress. However, when it is permitted to run out of control it can lead to poor performance, illness and eventually death — this is distress. Stress need never become distress if you regard its symptoms as an early warning sign which is there to make you aware of situations which threaten your well-being. Stress allows us to retire temporarily from a situation and is a sign that we need to take a break. The physical reaction to stress is what is known as a 'fight or flight' reaction; this means that hormones and chemicals are released into the body to help us fight or run away from the stressful situation. It is a throwback to prehistoric times when it was a means of survival and therefore of crucial importance. Animals without this system would be calmly grazing whilst a predator approached. Understandably they didn't live long enough to think about fighting or running away. As man evolved he developed the same fight or flight reaction to stress. However, the stressful situations in modern life are not created by predatory dinosaurs and stress needs different ways of being tackled. The internal reactions which aid the fight or flight syndrome are increased blood pressure, pulse rate, breathing, sweating, and muscular tension, none of which have any outlet in modern society. This process consequently places great strain on the body and mind. This stress syndrome feeds on itself because the more stressed we become the more tense, anxious and worried we are and this produces stress in itself. We end up in a vicious circle which leads to subsequent physical or emotional problems. There are many things that can cause us stress, although it's important to understand that stress, like beauty, is in the eye of the beholder. What may cause you stress may not concern me, and vice versa. Unfortunately there are many stresses common to most of us: we watch violence on television, often live in overcrowded circumstances and argue with a boss or our family. We may not have to contend with dinosaurs but the modern day dinosaurs — the tax-man or bank manager — are constantly with us. So we rarely find ourselves in a restful state. You may find yourself becoming anxious or irritable, you can't think straight and often suffer from headaches, sleeping problems or stomach upsets and in the longer term raised blood pressure or ulcers. The usual response is to drink more or to smoke more or to take tranquillizers, but none of these take the stress away, they merely hide the symptoms and allow a temporary escape.

There are typically four signs of stress:

1. Being anxious and finding it difficult to relax. Actually, anxiety can be divided into two groups here. (a) Anxiety learned from the past, from others, usually parents, and incorporated into the system. This is known in medical terms as free floating anxiety. (b) Specific anxiety related to present day situations such as coping with mortgages and traffic jams.
2. Becoming angry and irritable when things don't go as you want them to.
3. Worrying about things that worry won't help.
4. Experiencing difficulty in concentrating.

I will explore what causes stress and how much damage it can cause before explaining numerous techniques for leading a more relaxed life.

Attending to the signals of vague discomfort and minor ailments is rather like listening to an early warning system. If our present way of thought, living, emotions are reflected in our body, then these signals can make us aware of the possible need for change at the physical, psychological, or spiritual level.

Two doctors, Dr Peter Nixon, Consultant in Cardiology, Charing Cross Hospital, and Dr David Peters, a GP from Hayes, have suggested how attention to some of these bodily signals might be directed, when we are, to quote Dr Nixon, 'In the nether land between being well and not having brewed up specific illness.' Dr Nixon's work with cardiac patients has led him to develop what he calls the Human Function Curve Check List. We need an appropriate degree of arousal (wakefulness) to achieve anything. If we get too relaxed all we can do is sleep! But the pressures of outer life or inner conflict can force us to become so aroused that we develop a 'hair trigger' and become emotionally fragile, tired but sleepless, and, striving to cope, can only get more aroused and accomplish less! At such a point in life, having gone beyond healthy fatigue and chosen to or been obliged to ignore feelings and needs, each extra demand becomes a burden inexorably decreasing overdrawn reserves of energy. With no clear way of earning more, we slide into exhaustion and disease.

The Human Function Curve Check List.

Am I on the downslope?

Because too much is demanded of me?
Because I cannot say 'no' when I should?
Because I am not sufficiently in control? Can't cope?
Too angry, too tense, too upset, too irritable, too indignant?
Too much 'people-poisoning'?
Too many time-pressures? Too impatient?
Because I am not sleeping *well* enough to keep well?
Because I am not keeping fit enough to stay well?
Because I am not balancing the periods of hard effort with adequate sleep and relaxation?
Because I am out of real energy and using sheer will-power to keep going?
Because I am infallible, indispensable, indestructible, immortal?

Change is the situation most likely to cause stress to us because it usually means some disruption of our relationships or stabilizing influences in our life. An apparently minor change can cause considerable feelings of helplessness or hopelessness. It is not so much that a quantitative rating or value is attached to change or crisis but rather that your ability to adapt to change is important. If you perceive a threat in your ability to cope with change, stress will occur; it is therefore a matter of positive or negative expectancy more than anything else. Studies have shown that for people who were chronically ill, high stress and repeated crises were related to a life of unfulfilled expectations. Often these people felt that they had been somehow prevented from achieving what they were really capable of achieving. We need to learn to be flexible in our attachment to other people, groups and goals and to be able to change readily and easily to other relationships when established ones are disrupted.

In 1969 two American medical researchers, Thomas Holmes and

Richard Rahe, studied the effects that changes in life brought about in 5000 patients. They looked for specific events which seemed to precipitate patient illness and discovered very significant patterns. When a number of changes occurred in life during a relatively short period of time the patient was more likely to become ill. They were able to list the greatest stresses that you and I are likely to encounter in our everyday lives and give them a quantitative value.

This social readjustment scale, as it's now called, is used by psychologists and stress counsellors to help provide an early warning of possible stress-related illness. Obviously it can only give a fairly rough idea of the stress people are under and help them to make an educated guess as to how bad its effects may be because it cannot take into account the sort of person they are. This is their list:

Life event	Score
Death of spouse	100
Divorce	73
Marital separation	65
Prison or mental hospital confinement	63
Death of a close family member	63
Major injury/illness	53
Marriage	50
Being made redundant	47
Marital reconciliation	45
Retirement	45
Major change in health or behaviour of family member	44
Pregnancy	40
Sexual difficulties	39
Adding to family (through birth, adoption, elderly parents moving in)	39
Major business readjustments	39
Major change in financial state	38
Death of a close friend	36
Change in line of work	36
Major change in number of arguments with spouse	35
Taking on mortgage for purchasing home, business etc.	31
Foreclosure on a mortgage or loan	30
Major change in job responsibility	29
Son/daughter leaving home	29
Trouble with in-laws	29
Outstanding personal achievement	28
Wife beginning/ceasing work outside home	26

Beginning/ceasing formal education	26
Major change in living conditions	25
Revision of personal habits	24
Trouble with boss	23
Major change in working hours/conditions	20
Change in residence	20
Change to a new school	20
Major change in recreation	19
Major change in church activities	19
Major change in social activities	18
Taking on a loan of under £5000	17
Major change in sleeping habits	16
Major change in number of family get-togethers	15
Major change in eating habits	15
Holidays	13
Christmas	12
Minor violations of the law	11

Holmes and Rahe claim that if during the course of the preceding year you can accumulate a score of over 300 points your chance of a serious health problem developing in the next two years is 80 percent. If your score is between 150 and 300 points you have a 50 percent chance of serious illness within the next two years. The risk drops to 33 percent for a score of below 150 points. When I have used this chart in my seminars I have often found that there have been people with a relatively high level of stress although it has done very little damage to their health — simply because they're taking time to relax and to unwind. By the same token there have been many people who have scored a relatively low figure on this chart for whom stress has had negative consequences because they're not doing anything about it. The important point to remember is that if you have a high score it does not necessarily mean that you will become ill. What is important is your ability to *adapt* to these changes and to learn relaxation.

Barrie Hopson has compiled a list of questions to ask yourself in order to help cope with changes:

Know yourself, your feelings and attitudes. What do you stand to gain or lose? How can you help yourself to cope?

Know your new situation — what does it involve? How should you behave? Can you try aspects of it out in advance?

Know other people who can help by providing you with a sense of your own worth, someone to talk to, information, a perspective on your troubles.

Learn from the past. How did this happen? Has anything like it happened before? If so, how did you (or others) cope?

Look after yourself. You're the most important person you know, so keep fit, eat sensibly, talk positively to yourself.

Let go of the past. What's done is done — don't brood. Vent your anger constructively.

Set goals and make action plans. Decide what's best for you and work out how to do it. Think of alternatives.

Look for the gains you've made. Think positively. What have you gained or learned? What new opportunities have emerged?

There are a number of symptoms associated with 'not feeling well' that have genuine causes often linked to stress. Typically they are:

Tired, but can't get proper sleep.
Breathless, though fit.
Not yourself, but can't do anything about it.
Anxious, but not clear why.
Angry at no one in particular.
Vague aches and pains.
Feel like post-flu, but have not had it.
The harder you try, the less you achieve.

These sorts of symptoms, which represent neither 'wellness' nor 'disease' may represent an opportunity to re-evaluate the way we experience ourselves. Don't ignore it. Do take seriously those changes that may have occurred recently in your life and which we looked at on the Holmes/Rahe stress list. Look at your frustrations, anger, grief, fear. Hiding unacceptable emotions from yourself is exhausting and a drain on physical energy. Is the problem connected with your inability to slow down? To take a rest? To be indispensible? Do you know why you need to be indispensible or perfect? Is the message of tiredness or exhaustion about resting and re-evaluation? What happens if you ignore the experience? Who can help you to rest or to re-evaluate? What skills might be needed? Who can teach you? How can you prevent further episodes? Illness can, therefore, be about un-freedom, inflexibility, insensitivity. Its 'cure' may be through developing the opposite to these.

Often illness strikes in the middle of a crucial time in your life such as dissatisfaction in a job or relationship, or following retirement, divorce, etc. It is as if the illness is a symbol of a need to heal your life, to change from a mode of living no longer valid which up until now may have been prevented by your own fear of the unknown. Now matters are taken out of your hands and everything pales into insignificance as your own well-being becomes the focal point.

Every individual has two options open to them in just how they will allow the cancer, or any illness, to change their own personal life: either they can choose to sink into a despondent, no-hope state of apathy or, alternatively, they can choose to rally a warrior spirit and fight with positive optimism. One's own mental attitude is of the utmost importance, and one's ability to deal with illness can also take the line of passiveness, a letting go, allowing the body to take rest; accepting the situation rather than resisting it. This is not the same as giving in but merely allowing body and soul time to recover its own energies rather than frenetically keeping on the go — feeling that relaxing for one moment will give the illness the edge. A balance has to be reached, for over exertion leads not to health and well-being but to extra stress and fatigue.

Studies on the attitudes of cancer patients have found consistently that they have an attitude to life which has no sense of the future, tending to dwell on past misfortunes and to lack confidence. Often the person has suffered severe emotional disturbances in early childhood and frequently this is connected with relations with the parents and/or the break-up of the family unit, through divorce or death of either parent, the child subsequently experiencing a great sense of loss and rejection.

Lawrence LeShan who has conducted some of the most extensive work concerning psychological factors in cancer, concluded after collecting information from a group of 250 patients with malignant disease that certain psychological patterns were clearly characteristic.

1. A lost relationship prior to the cancer being diagnosed. (In 1926 Jungian analyst Dr Elida Evans wrote in *A Psychological Study of Cancer*, which was based on her observations of one-hundred cancer patients, that many were found to have lost an important emotional relationship prior to their cancer; identity investing to the extent of having few internal resources to fall back upon when this other figure was removed. It is therefore probably no coincidence that six out of the top ten factors listed in the Holmes/Rahe stress scale relate to another human being, our relationship with the other and how we perceive and handle it: death of a spouse, divorce, separation, death of a close family member, marriage, marital reconciliation, etc.)

2. Inability to express hostility in own defence.
3. Feelings of unworthiness and self-dislike.
4. Tension in relationship with parents.

Carl and Stephanie Simonton gave similar predisposing factors:

1. Strong tendency to hold resentment and inability to forgive.
2. Tendency toward self-pity.
3. Poor ability to develop and maintain meaningful long-term relationships.
4. Very poor self-image.

Drs Greer and Morris from Kings College Hospital, London, established from interviewing 160 women between 1973 and 1974 with undiagnosed breast lumps about to undergo a biopsy, that the sixty-nine whose biopsies transpired to be malignant suppressed anger and bottled up other emotions more than the women whose lumps turned out to be benign.

A number of retrospective studies suggest that those with a diminished ability to express their feelings are more prone to cancer. In February 1986 a four-year study of 2163 women reporting for breast screening (which was conducted jointly in Manchester, Huddersfield and London and headed by Professor Carey Cooper), statistically linked breast cancer to stress and the individual's ability to deal with it. The study also showed that those more likely to develop breast cancer are women who are reluctant to show their emotions, are less competitive, aggressive, and more withdrawn.

Two significant constants have been found in a number of research studies, these being that cancer patients appear to experience considerable difficulty in their personal relationships as a function of their disease, and that there is apparently a positive connection between the quality of a person's relationships with others and the ability to cope with illness. Observing 120 cancer patients having undergone a mastectomy during 1976 for the three- to four-month period following diagnosis it was reported in an article in *The American Journal of Medical Science* in 1977 dealing with post-mastectomy depression that the presence of strong interpersonal support was viewed as a psychosocial asset that contributed substantially to successful coping.

There are those in whom the disease appeared to be under control but recurred many years after the primary cancer had been removed. Those cells which had been present in the body since the time of initial diagnosis and had been controlled successfully for some time suddenly make their presence known — why? The implication is that the person's immune system which had been able to control the malignant cells has for some reason stopped or malfunctioned. This is now generally accepted to have a direct link to stress, trauma or psychological strain, which has sparked off the cancer's re-emergence by breaking down the immune system's fighting power. A lot of the worry and tension in our everyday lives we create ourselves in our expectations of others, misgivings, misconceptions, wounded pride, hurt feelings, lack of communication, etc., and these all tend to fester into an open sore, full of anger, sadness and emotional pain. But there is a better way out of this emotional disease. Through meditation and relaxation we can come to still both mind and body, and apart from effectively coping with stress in a positive way it also helps us to avoid unnecessary fatigue, giving the body's own natural healing forces a chance to function more efficiently. Being still, breathing correctly and relaxing with an open and receptive attitude are all that is needed. By breathing out all accumulated fear, worry and stress and deepening the breath in the abdominal region a calming effect is created enabling a deeper level of relaxation to be reached.

Before I discuss these healing methods though, let us take a look at worry, which is perhaps the most easily understood form of stress. Worry never solved any situation and it invariably makes you feel worse. So why worry? You may find the following listed suggestions helpful if you are a worrying type. They were originally published in Australia by the New South Wales Department of Health.

1. *Talk it out.* Share your worry with someone else; go halves on it. It's amazing how much better you feel if you can talk to somebody.
2. *Write it out.* Try writing it on paper and then cutting it down to size. If a worry goes round and round in your mind it seems much bigger than it is when you have actually written it down in words on paper.
3. *Laugh it off.* Dissolve it with humour. Let's face it, it's more difficult to be worried if you're laughing.
4. *Shrug it off.* Try raising your shoulders and then dropping them; relax yourself. This works because often when you are worried the tension goes straight to your neck and your shoulders and you find yourself with hunched shoulders.
5. *Breathe through it.* Breathe slowly from your abdomen and calm yourself. The more worried you become the worse your breathing gets, and the worse your breathing gets the more tense you feel. If you start to control your breathing by breathing slowly and easily,

that will make you feel much better.

6. *Balance it.* Count your blessings and be thankful because, no matter how bad your situation at the moment, there must be something good in your life and it's easy to focus on the negatives rather than some of the positives. Try balancing it with some of the positive things that are going on. Add up the possible good consequences of your situation.

7. *List practical options.* Don't just sit there and worry about it. Worrying is not going to solve the situation at all. Weigh up the situation, make a decision and act. Do something about it.

8. *Distance it.* See the situation from five years ago and then, if you can, project yourself five years forward. Once you can see your problem, from behind and from in front, you sometimes get a completely different perspective on it.

9. *Delay it.* Find a time, perhaps first thing in the morning or last thing at night, when you are going to sit down and do nothing except worry about this problem. When you've worried about it for fifteen minutes say 'Right, that's the end of it, I've worried about it enough, I've given it sufficient time for today, I'm not going to think about it again!'

10. *Work it off.* Do something physical. Go and clear your head. Too many of us are sedentary: we drive to work, sit in an office, come home and sit in front of the television. We never actually do any exercise and if you're worried you start to get tense. Walk the dog, cut logs, take up aerobics, anything like that where you are doing something physical because it will help you.

11. *Win through it.* Close your eyes and instead of imagining the worst, see yourself winning, see yourself beating the problem and imagine yourself coming through it.

12. *Cancel it.* Think positive thoughts; neutralize the negative.

13. *Exaggerate it.* Imagine the very worst that can happen and then ask yourself, 'how likely is that?' The funny thing is, often when you've imagined your worry as the very worst that can happen, when you actually get back to the worry in reality it seems far smaller than it was originally.

14. *Hold it.* Say to yourself 'Stop, pause'. When you pause, take a fresh look, because often you spend your time worrying about a situation, but never think about anything else. Sometimes if you take a break from worrying about it — if you go and do something else — you think about something else; when you go back to it afterwards you'll suddenly see a completely different solution which had not occurred to you before.

15. *Escape it*. Notice something nice around you and get into the present. Live in the present. Don't spend your entire life filled with remorse, or guilt about what has happened in the past and don't worry about the future, because in the process you miss the most important time of all — the present. You can spend your life filled with remorse about what's happened in the past and worrying about what hasn't happened in the future and in the process forget to live.

16. *Transfer it*. Make it somebody else's problem, at least until you're stronger. This happens often with my patients; perhaps they've become ill because there's been some great worry or stress in their lives, or perhaps it's somebody who has financial problems and is trying to sort themselves out. Make it somebody else's problem — ask an accountant or somebody else to sort out your financial problems, at least until you are strong enough to deal with it yourself.

17. *Reverse it*. Do the very opposite and see how that feels.

18. *Welcome it*. Do the opposite and see how that feels.

19. *Pincer it*. Think like a doer and act like a thinker.

There are four methods of relaxation which I recommend or use with my patients. By relaxation I do not mean sitting slumped in front of the television or sleeping. It is a positive skill which must be learnt and practiced regularly to achieve its special effect upon the mind and body. A short period of ten to twenty minutes a day of proper relaxation has been shown to lower blood pressure, slow down the heart rate, overcome fatigue and improve concentration as well as relieving a variety of common symptoms which may be due to tension, such as backache and headaches. Learning how to relax properly can benefit us all. Relaxation methods take time to learn and may take several weeks to work out, but once mastered their beneficial effect increases and there is of course no risk of becoming dependent.

The mental imagery technique

Sitting in a comfortable position or reclining in a well-supported position become aware of your face. Are you frowning or clenching your teeth? Both are signs of muscle tension caused by over-arousal. Make a conscious and deliberate act of clenching your teeth, frowning and pouting with your lips. Screw up your eyes then relax those muscles for a moment, repeating the motions. You can repeat this as you move down your body by forcing your shoulders down towards your feet and then relaxing them. Clench your fists away from your body and then curl up your toes and finally relax those muscles.

    What follows is a typical relaxation exercise of the kind that I use with many of my patients, although of course it is most effective if someone can speak it for you, perhaps with some gentle, soothing music in the background.

'I'd like you to relax your tongue by placing it gently behind your lower front teeth. Part your teeth just a fraction and let your lips touch ever so lightly.

'As you close your eyes withdraw your eyesight. Your eyes are closed and deep, deep in their sockets. Don't impose on your eyes, just let them go as long as they are completely at ease. Withdraw your hearing and feel all noise fade away.

'Breathe in deeply and fill your lungs. As you exhale you sink deeper and deeper into yourself; inhale and sink deeper and deeper and deeper into yourself; inhale and withdraw more and more. You are now in a contented frame of mind. Your body is very heavy, at ease, and warm. Listen to your heart; it's beating steadily and regularly. As you listen to your heart you feel its beat in the whole of your body. It feels as if you're on a boat in a calm, calm sea with the water lapping, gently rocking you. The inhaling and exhaling is like the waves, they are gently rocking you. The rocking continues in your mind and as you rock one after the other the negative emotions are dropping away from you: frustration, sorrow, depression, heartache, worries, resentment and anything else. You feel serene and contented; you feel so wonderful you'd like the whole world to enjoy it with you. And out of the depths of your heart rises a great lightness, and you feel it flow in a continuous steady stream through your whole body. And all the time you feel lighter and lighter, drifting away into a state of peaceful relaxation.

'Imagine now that you are standing at the top of some stairs; in fact there are ten steps in all. Slowly I'd like you to count from one to ten going down one step with each number and breathing out with each number with each step down. One, two, three, four, five, six, seven, eight, nine, ten. At the bottom of the stairs is a very special garden. Imagine that you stroll around this garden, feeling more at peace, more and more tranquil. Allow the world at the top of your stairs to just drift away. The grass beneath your feet feels like a cushion, the fresh air is scented with flowers, the Sun feels warm and everywhere is peace and serenity. Allow the conscious, questioning part of your mind to drift away — it has no role in this garden. This is a passive garden which allows the back of your mind to drift into view. As you stroll slowly through this garden you come across an overhanging rock over which a stream of water is gently tumbling into the shallow pool below. Reach out and touch the water. It feels fresh and cool. The silvery drops of water catch the Sun's rays and throw a pattern of dappled light across you. I want you to imagine now that you are standing under this gentle waterfall, allowing the cool water to flow over your body. As the water passes over you, imagine that all your muscles relax, relax in this stream of gently cascading water. Become aware now of your hands, wriggle your fingers, bring awareness back to your feet. I'd like you to blink your eyes and stretch. Feel on top of the world, and be aware of this feeling of peace, well-being and release from pain which will remain with you.'

Breathing

Here is a familar scene. You are driving along in your car when someone else pulls out from a side turning, apparently oblivious of your approach. For a moment a collision seems inevitable, and as you slam on the brakes your body suddenly goes into a state of alert in anticipation of imminent danger; then at the last moment the collision is avoided, but you're still left with the stress that it created. What do you do? Quite simply you control your breathing.

At that point you have got quite a lot in common with an athlete like Jeff Capes or a mother during childbirth because both have learnt a variety of techniques for using deep breathing to decrease overall anxiety and pain. These are positive uses of controlled breathing, but unfortunately too many people tend to follow the example of RAF pilots during the last war. One of the biggest problems for the RAF at that time was the loss of men and machines through battle fatigue of the pilots. What most baffled the RAF was the lack of pattern in breakdowns. Some pilots cracked up after a small number of flights whilst others doubled or tripled the statistic for no apparent reason. There were a few pilots who just didn't seem to get unduly affected by strain and never broke down.

Most people would consider this as normal — different personalities, different reactions. But in the case of the fighter pilots there was more to it. Pilots had to pass the most vigorous tests and nothing was left to chance as the pilots, as well as the machines, took a long time to replace. All the men had similar reactions to the tests and therefore basically had a lot in common. Then, near the end of the war, the researchers found a very peculiar item which was checked, rechecked and stood up to all the tests. Those pilots who had the longest intervals between exhaling and inhaling again were practically immune to stress; the shorter the interval the quicker the breakdown.

Hyperventilation is the term used to described over-breathing — many people breathe too rapidly or too deeply for their body's requirements.

This produces a decrease in carbon dioxide in the blood, and many symptoms may result from this. Learning to breathe correctly, that is at a suitable rate using the diaphragm rather than the chest, may make dramatic changes to how you feel. This usually requires some instruction from a qualified physiotherapist as hyperventilation is often a long-standing habit. Doctors are finding this to be related to a multitude of illnesses which were previously thought to be due to other causes.

Anxiety is greatly increased if the breathing pattern is incorrect and just altering this pattern may change someone from a nervous wreck to a competent relaxed person. In order to tell if you are a hyperventilator, stand up and place one hand on your chest and the other on your abdomen. Breathe normally and notice if the upper or lower hand is moving. If your upper hand is moving you are breathing incorrectly and this may be an underlying cause as to why you have unexplained symptoms. If your lower hand is moving and your upper chest hand is still then you are using your diaphragm, which is the correct organ for breathing at rest. The chest is used for extra oxygen as in the fight or flight response.

The human body is remarkably adaptive and resilient. Human beings can survive for a long time without food, and for several days without water, but without air life ceases in only a matter of minutes. The fact is that every cell in our body needs a continual charge of oxygen in order to carry out its assigned function. The job of breathing is to supply this energy to the bloodstream, but since it's been happening automatically for every moment of your life you have probably given very little attention to it. Yet without it everything stops. When the air is clear, your lungs strong, your body relaxed and your mind at peace, you experience total well-being; unfortunately this ideal is seldom realized. Breathing may be likened to the functioning of the old-fashioned blacksmith's bellows — lift up the handles, open the bellows and air is sucked in; press down, flatten the bellows and air rushes out. The components of the process here are those of volume and pressure. As the volume of the bellows increases the internal pressure decreases, creating a vacuum effect which draws in the outside air. When the bellows collapse the volume decreases and the increasing internal pressure forces the air back out again.

Every cell, every muscle, bone and organ in your body needs oxygen. When part of you is ailing the whole organism is thrown out of balance. Vigilant red blood corpuscles rush to the aid of the injured or diseased member. Since it is the oxygen you inhale which provides the energy to the cells it naturally follows that these cells need to be charged to their fullest potential in order for healing to occur. It has long been known that pain is intensified by the anxiety which accompanies a threatening situation; fear causes the body to tense itself, which is a spontaneous reaction to the need to fight or run away. So what we have is a two-stage process — fear giving rise to tension and tension increasing pain. Using the breath to limit tension will help to quiet both the fear and the pain.

The intuitive wisdom used by parents of young children provides us with a good example. The child who has been crying and gasping for breath is told to calm down and take a deep breath. The mother knows that a child's pain is worsened by the scare and the sight of blood. Panic reactions generally involve the same gasping or fast shallow breathing pattern, and bringing it to the attention of the injured party can immediately change the level of anxiety. In order to use this in a crisis situation for yourself it helps to be attuned to it on a regular basis.

Next time you feel agitated check your breathing; the chances are that if you really get tense or anxious your breathing becomes shallow and rapid — you are hyperventilating. Slowing your breathing down is one of the quickest ways of reversing the effects of stress.

Dr Claude Lumm, formerly consultant chest physician at the Papworth Hospital near Cambridge, who pioneered the study of hyperventilation in this country, feels that chronic over-breathing can lead to anxiety states which in turn can lead to heart conditions. He showed that deep breathing exercises could on their own reduce anxiety by considerable degrees in over-stressed patients.

To practise deep breathing, he suggests that you say a number and then a three syllable word, to equal one second. Although it might sound silly you could say, for example, one el-e-phant, two el-e-phant. This can be practiced anywhere, and in time it can become an automatic response to a stressful situation.

Let us start with a breathing exercise which lengthens the breath and establishes a sense of peace.

'I'd like you to sit or lie in a comfortable position; make sure that neither your arms nor legs are crossed. Surrender your weight to the chair or the floor. If your body is comfortable its aches and twinges won't distract your attention. Make sure that your back is straight and that your shoulders are relaxed. Gently close your eyes now and make sure there is no frown between your eyebrows.

Inhale now to a count of four and exhale to a count of eight. Make sure that your shoulders really are relaxed and establish the rhythm of your breath. In — four pulse beats; out — eight pulse beats.

'Keep your mind occupied now with the gentle ebb and flow of your breathing. Be aware of the fact that you not only take in breath, life force, but that you give out in double measure.

'Bring your attention to your nose and imagine what the air looks like as it enters your body here. Imagine that you follow its path down into your lungs and that you see it swirling around. Now imagine it as it moves back up and out; as it leaves tell yourself that it is taking with it tension or pain or illness. With every breath you take in, the healing energy is swirling into your body. Bring your awareness now to the centre of your abdomen; imagine that there is a little hole there through which you are now breathing; visualize the oxygen coming in and swirling around your abdomen and lower back area and then flowing out again. As you exhale through this tiny hole, all tension or pain is being carried away and released. Now focus on a point in the centre of your chest, close to your heart. Visualize a tiny door opening there and imagine that as you inhale the air pours through that little doorway into your chest and right through your upper body into your heart. Watch it swirling around and carrying away tension as you exhale. Imagine all anxiety and stress being released as you exhale. With every breath you take you are breathing in life force and healing energy.

'Imagine now that the point of your breathing has moved to the centre of your forehead. Breathe from here, releasing any tightness in the muscles of your face. Imagine that your head is full of cobwebs and as you inhale they are all cleared out. Continue to breathe naturally and begin to stretch your whole body.

'As you slowly open your eyes be aware that this feeling of well-being will remain with you for the rest of the day.'

Exercise

Psychologically exercise provides an opportunity to escape for a while from preoccupation about your job. It can also provide an opportunity to release bottled up feelings. Dr Alexander Leaf of Harvard Medical School has recently made extensive clinical and social observations on very old people in several parts of the world. His studies have led him to believe that longevity is connected not only with a rather frugal diet but also with vigorous and continued physical activity. Exercise is one of the most simple ways of reducing the effect of stress because it has the effect of improving general body fitness and resistance to illness. It strengthens the muscles, and by accelerating the general metabolism and increasing our oxygen intake it maintains active growth processes in all of our body's cells. In relation to stress it functions in a number of useful and specific ways.

Ancient yogis knew many things that scientific research is now 'discovering' for itself. It is a fact that 'What you don't use, you lose'. Doctors now encourage people recovering from heart attacks to engage in a gradual, safe exercise programme. Relaxation techniques are taught in hospitals to help all sorts of conditions from pregnancy to anxiety states, insomnia to asthma. It is not so unusual for doctors to recommend yoga or to practise it themselves. The medical profession is keen to encourage older people to keep moving. It is particularly important (though perhaps hardest of all) for the arthritis sufferer. Many elderly people have said that they have found yoga especially helpful for this problem, though to be effective practice must be regular (little and often is best) and must never be done while a joint is inflamed.

I have often advocated yoga as an excellent form of exercise. You may wonder why yoga rather than, say, jogging. The ancient practice of yoga (originating centuries BC) is ideal for elderly people — indeed for those of any age who have some minor or even severe disability. As we get older health problems often crop up — a 'tricky' hip, breathing difficulty, a heart condition perhaps, or arthritis. Then we may be afraid to exercise in case we harm ourselves or aggravate the condition. There may be the feeling that we are generally stiffening up, or are simply 'not as young as we were' and really don't fancy all that vigorous leaping around that 'keep fit' exercises seem to involve. Yoga works so well because its slow, smooth movement can be adapted to every individual. If your arm will only lift to shoulder height, that's OK, you work at that level. There is time to find the fine line between effort and strain, without a sense of competition or feeling that you have to 'keep up'. And yoga is more than physical exercise. Good classes still include attention to posture and breathing. Mental exercise comes into it too — concentration, visualization and of course relaxation. It is a complete, balanced and, above all, gentle system.

Laughter

In 1986 a symposium was held in Toronto, Canada, for doctors, nurses and therapists on the healing power of laughter and play. Not only were the physiological benefits for the patient put forward, but it was also stressed that those on the other side, doctors and nurses, must develop their own sense of humour. One practitioner of laughter therapy is American physician Dr Patch Adams who runs seminars on how to be a nutty doctor! According to one French doctor, Pierre Dachet, laughter can deepen breathing, expand blood vessels, improve circulation, speed tissue healing and stabilize many body functions. In short it acts as a powerful drug. It has been noted by some French researchers who termed laughter 'stationary jogging' that those who laugh a lot are less prone to digestive orders and stomach ulcers. This research has led to a new form of therapy in France called 'jovialisme'. Developed mainly by French-Canadian Andre Moreau, whose own studies have led him to the conclusion that laughter speeds up the healing process, in America too doctors are now beginning to realize that laughter can be one of the most effective ways of promoting healing. One French lady, Julie Hette, has even made a career out of being a professional laugher — you can hire her for 300 francs an hour and she will guarantee to make you dissolve in helpless laughter. Humour therapy is becoming so accepted as a valid form of treatment in America that some hospitals are now starting to set aside a special laughter room for their patients.

Recent research has shown that people who can laugh at themselves cope with obstacles far more effectively and rebound more quickly than those who simply cannot smile at misfortune. An American counsellor, Harvey Mindess, specializes in the use of humour as a healing tool. He believes that humour is a very great coping mechanism. When a client is very anxious about something he tries to get them to break out of their anger or fear by laughing at themselves. The advantage of humour is that you can safely release a lot of repressed thoughts that perhaps normally you would not have the chance to express. Those who keep their sense of humour can deal with more of life's problems and release pent-up tension in a pleasant way. One of the things that has always struck me, not only in my work but generally, is the fact that some people are always very serious. I think it is because schools and society teach us how to work but not how to play.

Another word that might substitute for the word play, could perhaps be the word 'recreation'. The dictionary defines recreation thus: 'make new, revitalize, inspire with life and energy'. I believe that playing is a form of self-healing and nourishment, and because we don't take very much time playing as adults, we often become serious. That in turn, affects our health.

Playing is an attitude rather than something which you actually do. It's an attitude, if perhaps you are lucky, that turns the mundane into something rather more interesting and exciting. We usually define play with words like fun, sports, laughter and so on. But play can also be peaceful, relaxing, beautiful. Often one finds people who won't play games, because they say it's 'a waste of time'. It's only a waste of time if you see play that way. Society conditions us, over our whole view of play or games. We usually regard play as the opposite of work, something that must only be done in our spare time. Children can play but not adults — adults have got to be serious. Psychologists tell us that inside everyone of us is a child. They refer to that child as the child ego state, and they claim that this so-called child ego state has two faces. Inside everyone of us is a little child who is spontaneous, who delights, screams, stamps its feet, loves and hates. This is what the psychologists call the *natural child*. The other child is always dependent on other people's approval, whether from parents, from teachers, employers, friends or anybody sending messages about how they want that person to behave, and it will do almost anything to gain it. That child must adapt, so that the psychologists call this child the *adapted child*.

The adapted child performs, it obeys, it agrees and it works to incorporate the many and often conflicting parental messages in order to be 'good'. As we grow older the child within never leaves us, but what seems to happen is that the adapted child takes over and the natural child becomes suppressed. Most adult play is a manifestation of the adapted child rather than the natural child. What better example have you got really of the adapted child at play than a football team? When the adapted child plays there is often a time schedule, there is competition, there is organization, there is a specific environment, whether it be a football pitch or a pool table; you have got to wear the right costumes and have the right equipment. You have got to be very serious about it and there is a reward for hard work. My argument is that both competition and seriousness have a strong influence on our health.

I have met many people who regard life as a game: you win some you lose some. That is fine — but if you think that life is a game you must realize that there are winners and there are losers. It's good if you happen to be on the winning side. Winning brings praise, reward, and it means that you are better than somebody else. Being on the losing side, though, represents failure, inadequacy, being bettered by somebody else and it is undesirable. There is a strong link between playing and competition.

'If you fight, someone loses; if you love, everybody wins' is the philosophy of life that we need to adopt. We need to see life as an experience where everybody wins. Everybody *can* win if we love rather than if we are always fighting. There is an attitude which seems to permeate so many areas of society: 'If I'm not good enough to make the team, I'm not good enough'. This attitude influences so many areas of our life — business, education, politics, ways of recreation, etc. We always end up comparing and then wanting. The pressures that result from this attitude encourage a wide range of stress-related problems which often end with heart disease or cancer.

Sometimes I've worked with a patient who it seems is bored with life; there is nothing much for them to do and all they are interested in is waiting for the next pill. Sometimes I have asked them, 'Why don't you go out and do something? Why don't you learn something? Why don't you go and learn French or basket making or learn to play the piano? Do something to occupy your time.' Very often they will say 'What's the point? *I wouldn't be any good at it anyway.*' Too often we will only do something if we are going to be good at it and if we are going to beat somebody else. We seem to have lost sight of doing something for the enjoyment of it, and surely that is why so many people then take life so seriously. Nothing needs to be that serious.

The opposite of play is excessive seriousness, and one of the things that strikes me is the way that so many people, even within the so-called health movement, are so serious. Even the job of becoming healthy becomes serious with warnings about what to eat and what not to eat, what to do and what not to do! Seriousness permeates our entire approach to religion, education, family affairs, politics and life in general. When did somebody last say to you 'You've got to start taking this much more seriously.' Perhaps that's the cause of your problems. Seriousness creates anxiety and tension, seriousness creates judgement and fear and it seems now that even if we play we must be serious. Whatever breaks undue seriousness and opens us up to play and the natural child will bring recreation and self-healing.

There is the well-known account of a man called Norman Cousins who was the editor of the *New York Saturday Review*. In 1964 he had been diagnosed as suffering from a very serious illness which affected his body's connective tissues. He was lying in hospital and had been told that he had a one in 500 chance of survival. He was hardly able to move and was in intense pain, really just waiting to die, when he realized two things. First of all the pain medication was actually worsening the condition and secondly the hospital was a very depressing place to be. Against all medical advice he checked out of the hospital into a hotel and began what he called laughter therapy. Having read several classic books on stress he had become convinced that disease was fostered by the chemical change in the body produced by emotions, such as anger and fear. He wondered whether an antidote of hope, love, laughter and the will to live would do the opposite. He started to watch Marx brothers' films, sequences of *Candid Camera* and anything else that made him laugh. He found that after watching, for example, Candid Camera sequences and really laughing he had several hours of pain-free sleep. He also read humorous books, told himself jokes and continued with his laughter therapy. Slowly he regained control of his body and could move without excruciating pain.

He subsequently wrote a book about his experiences called *The Anatomy of an Illness*. Critics said his recovery was due to placebo. In the end, does that really matter? Recent research has now shown that our thoughts can trigger the release of chemicals into our body. Our brain produces substances called endorphins, which act as the body's natural pain-killers. We now know that laughter is one of the emotions which will actually work to release these endorphins into our blood. Maybe that is why somebody involved in an accident and suffering from shock will start laughing, because it is in fact releasing pain-killers into the bloodstream.

New research shows that a good, hearty laugh acts like a mini-workout, revving up the cardiovascular, respiratory and nervous systems. According to Dr William Fry, Associate Clinical Professor of Psychiatry at Stanford University School of Medicine, 'The latest studies suggest laughter may also be a phsycial release — that the increase in heart and blood pressure rates and the muscle vibrations induced by laughing are often followed by a feeling of enhanced relaxation.'

Reappraisal of feelings, needs and pressures can allow us to retreat and seek the healing rest that symptoms are pointing towards. Dr Peter Nixon has found that patients who recover from heart attacks successfully are willing to 'make an audit' of their life style and to modify it where necessary. It is the people with the 'Icarus Syndrome', who ignore the signals from their bodies and minds, and drive themselves to exhaustion and heart attacks. He summarizes the elements of basic care (which is mainly self-healing) in the acronym SABRES:

S   = Sleep — awareness of the quantity and quality required.
A   = Arousal — awareness and modulation of rage and struggle, despair and defeat.
B   = Breathing — awareness and control in place of hyperventilation, irregularities of rate and depth of sighing.
R   = Rest — achieving the ability to be still.
E   = Effort — recognizing and respecting the limits of salutary physical and mental effort.
S   = Self-esteem — linked with confidence and restored by close support and the successful employment of the other elements of basic care.

If you have been in the habit of ignoring or suppressing minor ailments, many of the ideas in this chapter may be quite a new concept to you. Remember that what perhaps starts as disordered function can develop into physical disease, so attending to stress can be true prevention.

It is not morbid, shameful, or self-centred to look after yourself in this way. It's quite OK!

3.

You can heal yourself

At my Centre in Bury St Edmunds I treat a wide variety of problems, although a majority of my patients are cancer sufferers. I ask that my patients be an active participant in their recovery. As we always tell prospective patients: if you want me to help you, you must be prepared to also help yourself. Unbelievably this quickly eliminates about 40 percent of those who contact us! Many of those we lose at that early stage are elderly people who perhaps are more set in their ways and are more resistant to change.

Of the people who actually come to our Centre, about one-third come for one or two treatments and I never see them again. There are a number of reasons, I believe, as to why this happens. Some of those in this category have problems which did respond very quickly to my healing. This is usually so of 'mechanical' problems such as bad backs or arthritic pain. Some perhaps did not like me — that's fair enough. I'm a firm believer that for healing to work successfully there has to be some understanding and rapport between healer and patient. Others perhaps really cannot believe that they can do anything to help themselves in spite of our guidance. Some I think, in spite of everything I tell them when they first contact me, are looking for an instant miracle. It may surprise you to learn that most of those who drop out at such an early stage are women.

Many women who come to the Centre work very hard to look after their husbands, bring up their children and maintain a home — it is a full-time job. However, when I explain that I would like them to devote fifteen to twenty minutes twice or three times each day to themselves they feel they do not have the time to do so. A difficult concept for some to grasp is that to some extent you have got to be selfish in order to recover. Many women in family situations are not accustomed to selfishness as they have become used to giving so much. Tragically, especially for those with life-threatening illnesses, if you do not devote time to yourself at this stage, you may not have so much time to devote to others later. Adéla Pickering, a psychologist and hypnotherapist, also points out that some women could be playing a martyr role with this behaviour.

Contrary to popular press myths, it is not necessarily neurotic women who go to healers! Our records show that those who follow through and maintain treatment in the longer term tend more often to be men. It may also be of interest to know that the average age of our patients is between thirty-five and forty.

Therefore, although it may seem to an outsider that I get good results with my patients, it must be remembered that I am working with mostly highly motivated people who are prepared to help themselves and who have filtered themselves from the start. I am also enthusiastic about my work and it is a well-established fact that an enthusiastic doctor gets better results than a non-enthusiastic colleague.

When a patient first arrives at the Centre they usually have three things working against them: fear, isolation and depression. This is where we start.

Most of my patients arrive in varying states of fear. The degree of fear generally correlates with the prognosis and/or life expectancy. Usually fear is doing as much, if not more, damage than the illness itself. Patients have sometimes told me on their first visit that they dread what will happen to them. Dread is negative expectancy. It is expecting the worst. Dread and fear can be a lethal combination — literally.

In any given situation where alternatives are available, a frightened person will usually anticipate the worst — the most fearful and negative choice. Removing or understanding fear is like taking off the brake whilst driving a car. It allows natural optimism and positive attitudes to play a greater role in your life. In our daily life we base our actions on the *probability* of events occurring with the knowledge that there is a remote *possibility* of negative situations arising. We take these negative possibilities into account but we don't let them dictate our lives. Walking down the street we are aware that there is a remote possibility of a slate falling off a roof but we don't stay indoors or wear a crash helmet. The probability is that all will be well so we follow that belief. Someone who has underlying fear often pushes negative possibilities into the probability category and acts as if they *are* a probability.

Fear is a paramount response when dealing with illness — on all sides. Overcoming the fear can be initiated by the four point approach Carl and Stephanie Simonton use in cancer treatment:

1. Be *aware* that fear *exists*.

2. *Express* that fear and seek *support* from others.
3. Seek any *information* that will enable you to gain *understanding* and *control* over it.
4. Having *dealt* with your feelings, *allow* yourself to go ahead and *enjoy* your life, experiences and activities.

These points were echoed in a report published by Dr Stephen Greer in *The Lancet* in 1975. Over a five-year period Dr Greer investigated the attitudes of sixty-nine women who had been diagnosed as suffering from early breast cancer. The patients' psychological feelings towards their disease were assessed three months after surgery. Typically there were four responses to the disease. There were those patients who would deny that their breast had been removed for cancer and would say things like, 'It wasn't serious, they just took my breast off as a precaution.' They neither showed nor reported any emotional distress. Another group showed fighting spirit, were optimistic, very interested in the disease and planned to do everything possible to beat it. 'I can fight it and defeat it' was a typical comment. These two groups of women were found to be twice as likely to survive than those who just accepted the diagnosis and just carried on with life as normal, or those who felt their life was finished and were emotionally very distressed.

In 1980 I participated in a pilot study in a pain control clinic of a hospital. The doctors were interested to assess what effect, if any, my healing abilities had on patients suffering from intractable pain. One of the consultants who had arranged the study had become interested in the role of mind over body after an experience with one of his patients, a middle-aged lady who had been admitted to hospital for exploratory abdominal surgery. Preliminary scans and X-rays had revealed a cancerous tumour but the doctors were uncertain as to its extent. Before surgery the lady had asked that she be kept fully informed of the findings of the surgery; the doctor agreed to this. During the operation it was found that the cancer was much worse than had been thought: it had spread to her liver, a kidney and had invaded her bowel. From their considerable experience the medical team believed that there was nothing that they could offer to treat her condition, except to give pain-killers if and when they were needed. They thought that she had about six months to live.

The first thing she asked her doctor upon coming round from the anaesthetic was about the prognosis. Although he had agreed to give her the full facts, he suddenly realized how difficult it was going to be, as previously she had been unaware of the severity of her problem. He explained that she was seriously ill, that the cancer had spread much further than he had initially believed, and that medically there was nothing more he could do except to give her pain-killers. 'I believe you have up to two years to live,' he told her.

In his opinion her best option was to go away and live every day as fully as possible, as if it were her last. She died within forty-eight hours. She did not die of the cancer but, in his opinion, of fear. That, he told me, is why the medical profession sometimes witholds full facts from a patient. They are placed in the unenviable position of having to decide how a patient will respond to very traumatic news. His experience was one that I have subsequently seen on many occasions: people either fight tooth and nail to beat the illness or they very quickly give up and die.

It is often claimed by the media that there is 'a cancer epidemic', although I would dispute this. I feel that there is an epidemic of fear about cancer which is not helped by the regular flow of publicity about the large numbers of people who die of it. Too often we neglect the fact that thousands of people each year *do* survive cancer because of medical intervention, complementary therapies and the sheer determination of the individual patient. However, this is not often given publicity. We are not helped either by the fact that certainly until fairly recently much of the advertising for funds, not only for cancer research but for many other serious and potentially life-threatening illnesses, has relied heavily on presenting a dark and gloomy picture. The point that some of my patients make is that if you only present the blackest statistics you are likely to foster a negative response to the disease. If, for example, a woman discovers a lump in her breast and is told by a consultant that she has cancer, having seen advertising suggesting that 'cancer is a killer disease' she is immediately at an emotional disadvantage.

The second thing working against many of my patients is a strong sense of isolation. Cancer in particular is a taboo subject and people are frightened or embarrassed to talk openly about it. 'At the present time cancer is taboo. It is not difficult to understand why there is such a universal fear of the disease. The public believes that it must end fatally . . .' That statement was included in a report on *Radiotherapy in the Diseases of Women* written in 1933, yet it could quite as easily have been written today. Cancer sufferers discover that people they had considered friends will avoid them if at all possible. Perhaps at one time in their life when they would value someone to talk to and someone to share their feelings with their friends suddenly become scarce. I feel that certainly in the West we tend not to know what to say to somebody who is diagnosed as having a serious and potentially killing disease.

Unfortunately it is my experience that this also tends to spill into family relationships, and the family will also avoid any direct reference to the illness for as long as possible. They feel perhaps that it is better to distract the patient's mind from the problem. The consequence is that the patient becomes emotionally stranded, desperately wanting to talk to somebody but meeting blank spaces once filled by friends or diversions in conversational topics from the family.

About one in five of my patients will, especially during their first healing session with me, start to cry and appear quite upset. Initially I made the mistake of believing that their distress was a sign of pain, but I later realized that more often crying is a *release* of pain. An American researcher at Stanford University, Dr William Frey, discovered recently that when we cry for emotional reasons our tears contain stress hormones and chemicals associated with stress. If someone close to you starts to cry because of the situation in which they find themselves, the great temptation, in true Western style, is to reach for the paper handkerchieves and tell them to 'pull themselves together'. But this is not necessarily the best thing to do as it may well only suppress the emotions and stress hormones for which crying is a natural safety valve. My experience is that those people who are able to freely express their emotions in such crises are far more likely to recover than those who habitually mask their real feelings and never really let go.

Depression is the third thing that works to my patients' disadvantage. We all have our ups and downs — life is like that. Very few people get by without having days when they feel dejected or down. I find that these feelings tend to become exaggerated within my patients. They forget that they used to have off-days before they were ill and every problem seems to relate to their illness. I can also quite understand that people feel depressed when they or a loved one are diagnosed with a serious illness from which there seems no escape route. Most of those with whom I work do climb out of their depressed state once they appreciate that there *is* something they can do and that they are not merely helpless victims.

Let me now explain the very simple reason why I tackle the fear, isolation and depression right from the start.

Cancer is a name given to a diverse group of diseases having one thing in common, that they grow and spread. It starts not when a single cell suddenly alters its behaviour pattern, but when a number of malignant cell changes occur more or less at the same time, rapidly growing and invading the surrounding tissues, glands and bloodstream. Once a malignant tumour is well-established it metastasises, meaning a germ cell breaks off from the tumour and travels through the bloodstream or lymphatic system to establish new sites for growth in other areas of the body.

Sir Macfarlane Burnet, Nobel Prize winner for work in immunology, has stated that there could be up to as many as 100,000 cells in the body becoming cancerous each day, but the average person's immune system deals effectively with destroying these cancer cells.

I see cancer, therefore, as having much in common with diseases like tuberculosis, the common cold and so on. We are continually exposed to many damaging agents both from within and from without, but it is only when we become susceptible to them that the disease actually develops. The patient has it within his power to get well and this is based on many factors — evidence from biofeedback, from the various meditative procedures and from experience with spontaneous remission. The patient possesses enormous potential to influence his or her own vital forces to affect any illness.

By allowing yourself to be frightened, isolated and depressed you are effectively helping the progress of the illness and reducing the efficiency of your body's natural ability to fight back. There are several methods that I have found useful in combatting this potential weak link.

Several years ago I noticed that my patients, if given the opportunity, would freely converse about their problems whilst sitting in my waiting room. Typically a patient whom I had treated on several previous occasions would be waiting for his appointment, feeling optimistic and happy that he was doing something for himself and finding improvement already, when a second patient entered the waiting room. By her poise and looks it would be apparent that it was her first visit to the Centre and the two would start talking. The first patient might ask why she had come to see me. It was then that they both found they had almost the same problem and both were in the same boat together. That is usually the first opportunity that the patient coming in for the first consultation has ever had to talk to somebody else in a similar situation. We frequently hear the comment: 'You don't realize what a relief it's been just to have somebody to talk to.'

I now believe that this is one of the areas in which practititioners in the medical profession go wrong, not through any fault of their own but because they are overloaded with patients seeking treatment for minor ailments who take the time that the doctor could otherwise devote to patients with more serious problems. I was once told by a doctor who practised within the National Health Service, but supplemented his income by doing a certain amount of private work, that he achieved better results with his private patients than with his State patients, even though the medical treatment given to each group was identical. The difference was directly attributable, in his opinion, to the fact that he could devote more time to his private patients. It was time, rather than medical skill, that they were paying for. Whether or not all doctors would agree with him, I don't know.

Anyway, I began to organize regular informal meetings during which patients could talk to one another about their illnesses, their hopes and fears, their treatment and anything else that they felt relevant. I quickly discovered that even if a patient would not necessarily accept my word about self-help, they certainly would do so once they had met somebody else who had benefited. It was at this point that I learnt of an important factor.

We might receive a letter written by a husband on behalf of his sick wife telling us that he is prepared to try anything, to take his wife anywhere, that cost within reason is no problem, etc. However, what the husband says in his letter and what he does in practice are often two entirely different things. He will certainly bring his wife to the Centre but he will not come in himself. Instead he sits in the local car park reading his newspaper or he goes for a drink at the local hotel bar. When his wife emerges some time later she may not be the same person mentally and emotionally that he left there. She is now more confident and inspired to fight. One can imagine the conversation in the car as they drive home. The husband will tell his wife how Mrs Smith had the same problem . . . The wife remembers Mrs Smith because she also, three years ago, had a malignant breast tumour. She had a successful mastectomy and was fine for eighteen months until she developed secondaries. She gradually deteriorated and five months ago she died. The husband, by reminding his wife about how somebody else got worse, has begun a very efficient undermining process.

Experience has taught me that very often the partner will behave in this way simply because he doesn't want to confront the reality of the situation. By ignoring it, he believes it's not actually happening. This is another manifestation of fear. When we attempt to change a patient's belief system, we must also deal with the belief systems of his friends and relatives. In *The Healing Family*, Stephanie Matthews Simonton states:

> Anger and depression tend to dissipate when we fully experience and express them. For many, learning to let out feelings will seem risky and frightening. One common feeling people with cancer face, and one they are likely to suppress, is fear about their illness. Some acknowledge their fear to themselves but hide it from family members in order not to burden them. This often results in the patient feeling isolated and alone. The spouse will sometimes do the same thing.

It is for this reason that we now suggest that, for the first visit at least, the patient be accompanied by their spouse, a family member or a close friend who will help and support them during their recovery. I suspect that often husbands, and sometimes wives too, are pleasantly surprised to discover for themselves exactly what I do and to realize that it is all based firmly on common sense. Undoubtedly the patient has a far greater chance of improvement when there is a loving and understanding family support. Those patients without that often do not fare so well.

Sometimes by working in this way I gain a useful insight into the cause of the illness. I remember a lady who had, she told us, been brought by her husband. She had a malignant tumour and he was prepared to help his wife in any way possible. I realized during my first consultation with her that she had a very pessimistic outlook and was looking for a near miraculous recovery after her session. I explained realistically and honestly what I felt she could expect and managed to persuade her to join our discussion group that afternoon together with her husband.

To my surprise she agreed to participate in this and I sat her across the room from her husband. Knowing that she was rather negative I placed her carefully between a couple of my most positive patients and forewarned them of her attitude. They therefore took a great deal of time to make conversation with her and to encourage her to fight the disease. They explained to her the benefits they felt they had derived from a special diet based on raw fruit and vegetables and they told her of a clinic where she could find out more information about it. Her face lit up and for the first time I saw her smiling. Then, from the other side of the room, the husband announced that if she wanted to go there she would have to go by herself and travel on a coach as it was too far for him to drive. I was speechless and when I later reread his letter I noted that he had said that he was prepared to take his wife anywhere, no matter what the distance. The conversation continued and another patient suggested that it was much easier to maintain such a strict diet if your husband or wife would join you on it. This proved to be the last straw for the husband who told his wife, in front of everybody else, that he liked his porridge every morning. 'You can go on that kind of diet, but count me out,' he told her. We never saw either of them again.

When illness hits one member of the family, each other member of that unit needs time to stop and evaluate what this will mean, not only to the patient but to all the family. Therefore, time is needed to work through fears and plan ways of coping, both as an individual and as a supportive member of the family group; the whole family combining as a team to support not only the patient, but also each other, and in so doing benefit themselves as well.

The Simontons recommend, at their Cancer Counselling and Research Centre in Dallas, Texas, that family members, particularly the husband, try imagery and learn relaxation techniques as well, both as a means of obtaining a better understanding of the practice, and also to relieve their own stress and tension. Many, in becoming involved in such practices along with the patient, find their common initial reaction of scepticism changes.

Close friends are essential to provide additional emotional support and comfort outside of the family unit — not only for the patient but also for others in the family, allowing them time away from illness to meet others in whose company they can relax and feel able to express their *own* thoughts and worries, aside of those of the wife, mother, daughter or whomever. There is a real need for all the family members to have their own interests and recreations; sacrificing one's own wants and needs will only generate later resentment toward the patient.

I was once told by a doctor that neither he nor I could make anybody better. All either of us can do, he explained, is to help get the patient's body into optimum condition to heal itself. I know that the people who benefit most from my healing, both physically and mentally, are those who are willing to help themselves by using techniques of relaxation and visualization and learning to take a positive attitude towards life. All healing ultimately comes from within yourself and your self-healing powers are already there, lying within you, waiting to be tapped. You are probably reading this book because you want to help yourself; you have that spark of positive health inside you.

It often comes as a surprise to people to be told that they *can* take charge of the way that they think. We are brought up with the idea that pills and injections from outside can cure physical illnesses; there ought to be something equally easy to cure emotional ones. We are also brought up with the feeling that we are the victims of the unpleasant thoughts and emotions that just arrive in our heads. This is made worse when what we think or feel is unacceptable to other people, who tell us that we shouldn't feel like that, we should pull ourselves together. That is not what I mean by positive thinking. Often a patient cannot snap out of their negativity that easily, and whilst trying to pull themselves together by pushing aside unpleasant thoughts they merely repress these thoughts, only to have them emerge again later on, adding to their feeling of helplessness.

Many of my patients have what psychologists call a poor self-image.

They are always running themselves down; they always think the worst of themselves; any compliment they receive is quickly rejected. In short they are their own worst enemy.

So how can you think positively, and how does it work? The first thing is to realize that your brain and the thoughts it produces are not your whole self. The brain can in fact be regarded as an excellent computer into which all kinds of information have been programmed from your birth onwards by parents, teachers, society, advertising and the media. Because it is *your* brain inside *your* head, it feels like *you*, and what it thinks feels real and truthful to you. If your computer-brain tells you that you are a worthless person you will probably agree with it, and thus add to the store of negative information which may have nothing to do with actual reality at all.

You are not a computer, or a set of conditioned reflexes; you are a human being who was given that computer to serve you, not to control you. Once you begin to see what is happening, you can start to change that computer programme. You can decide right now that the next time you find yourself thinking something negative about yourself, you will replace that thought with something positive. That may sound simple, but it really does work. Each time you choose to think a positive thought you are re-educating your computer-brain.

There is, however, a world of difference between positive thinking and self-deception. Positive thinking does not mean trying to fool yourself that everything is fine when it is not. Let us take an imaginary example. I may have a patient who comes for healing because of a breast tumour. After talking to her I discover that the young woman concerned is unhappy because she has no boyfriend and is unmarried. She may well have been fed a programme by her mother, friends or the media that women are only worth something if they have a man in their lives, and as long as she continues to believe that she will go on feeling worthless and depressed. Once she can recognize that her belief is simply an old tape that has got stuck, she can replace it with something more positive. It is here that she must be realistic. It is no good if she tries thinking, 'Next week I'm going to meet the man of my dreams', as she is likely to be disappointed. The positive thought in this situation would be, 'I am worthwhile whether I am alone or not.' This will have several effects. As with any positive affirmation it will break the circuit of negative thinking into which she has been trapped; it will call a halt to the production of damaging stress hormones caused by her anxiety, and the more she thinks it, the more she will *feel* like a worthwhile person. Something may well then happen that often occurs when people make this kind of change in their thinking. Having learned to value herself and lose her anxiety, the tumour begins to regress and the right partner may well appear in her life.

I also find that frequently the thoughts of my patients are more like a stream of constant self-criticism that they may not be fully aware of. Try listening to what you are telling yourself because once you can hear what you are saying you can start contradicting it. There is a remarkably simple exercise which can quickly change negative self-beliefs to positive ones. Make two lists of beliefs that you have about yourself: one of negative beliefs and one of positive beliefs. When my patients have carried out this simple exercise they often find that the positive list only contains three or four items whilst the negative list covers sheet after sheet! Have an objective look at the negative ones and ask yourself whether they are really founded in fact. They may seem to be simply because you have been listening too well to the tape playing in your brain. I remember a young man who brought me his lists; one of his negative beliefs was, 'I am no good at making friends'. I crossed it out and by changing a few words placed it on his positive list. 'I am willing to make more friends' I wrote for him. The situation may be the same for the moment but at least he is giving himself a totally different message about it rather than acting on his old belief as though it were an instruction.

When you have gone right through the negative list, changing each entry to positive beliefs, wherever possible tear-up or throw away the negative list. You have listened to your own self-criticism for long enough. Make several copies of the new list of positive self-beliefs and pin it all over your home so that whichever room you are in you will see it and reinforce it.

There is an extremely useful book by Cherry Boone O'Neill entitled *Starving for Attention*. The author, a young woman, is a daughter of the famous American singer Pat Boone, and the book is an account of how she overcame the slimmer's disease, anorexia nervosa, by using self-healing techniques. She describes how she was not only refusing to eat properly but also taking overdoses of laxatives in her attempt to lose weight. After a number of massive overdoses she was hospitalized and very nearly died. She was kept in hospital so that she could be encouraged to eat properly and not later induce vomiting to lose it again. After several weeks in hospital she was barely any heavier than when she was first admitted because, although she would eat meals under the watchful eye of nursing staff, she would then ask to go to the toilet where she was not supervised. Sticking her fingers down her throat she would return all the food. She makes an important point at this juncture in her book: the doctors treating her never asked why she was doing it. They were treating symptoms and not the root cause. Her life was eventually saved with the intervention of a psychologist, Ronald Vath.

Vath's first question was why was she starving herself. With the help of his counselling it soom became apparent that there were two fundamental causes. The first was that for all her life she had lived in the shadow of her famous father and had developed a poor self-image. She was never Cherry Boone, she explained. She had always been known as 'Pat Boone's daughter'. It always seemed to her that everyone's attention, time and love was devoted to her father whilst her own emotional needs were not fulfilled. She began to starve herself literally, but unconsciously, to gain attention. The second factor was that from an early age she had been encouraged to follow in her father's footsteps and she had been thrust into his TV shows. Her parents wanted her to sing and dance and she was quite happy to do so for some time. During her teenage years she became aware of the images of apparent female perfection presented in advertisements in women's glossy magazines. Comparing herself against these other images she decided she was too fat and began to exercise and diet. Tragically she lost control and developed anorexia.

Ronald Vath used the positive/negative beliefs technique as one of his tools for self-healing with Cherry Boone. She describes how she had no idea that she had developed such a poor self-image; almost everything she believed about herself was negative. She spent several days transforming her negative beliefs into positive ones which she pinned all over her apartment. Additionally, her husband reinforced by telling her positive things about herself every hour for several days. She recovered and later wrote a book of her experience.

It may not be easy at first and you may not believe the positive things you are telling yourself. Don't worry about that. It may take a while to reprogramme your brain. Treat it as an exercise, a new skill to be learned, even a game. Do not expect to succeed at it the whole time, or you will simply find another reason for criticizing yourself when you fail. But if you take, say, five minutes in every hour thinking positive thoughts, you will be taking a major step in turning around the whole pattern of your thinking.

Once you begin to see that you *can* change your thoughts you will perhaps start to see that a whole number of things that had been damaging your health can be viewed in a different way. Facts are facts, but you have a choice about how you interpret them. Once you can see that, a whole new world of freedom lies ahead of you.

Occasionally the cause of illness in one of my patients may not be very specific. Rather, they have a general feeling that there is something wrong with life; perhaps it has not turned out the way they thought it would when they were young; or perhaps, if they are young, it is not the way they think it *should* be, full of fun, love, success and excitement. People are not helped by the fact that the media, films, television and especially advertising often present some sort of ideal life that we all ought to be enjoying. If you look at the real world you will see that very few people are living 'ideal' lives. But the happiest people are those who maybe recognize that life is not always perfect and that they are responsible for their own happiness and do not take it personally when things are unsatisfactory.

Comparing life as you think it ought to be with life as it really is and blaming yourself or others when things do not fit in with your ideal is quite a good way of getting depressed. Some of the people who come to the Centre like to use blame. 'This would never have happened if my daughter hadn't married that dreadful boy.' Blame never helps any situation or solves any problems so it is best to forget about it. Have a look at the situation, whatever it is, and see if you cannot find another way of looking at it. Perhaps the husband or wife that you feel is neglecting you just as badly needs your love and attention. Perhaps you have decided that you are a failure because you have not passed an exam or you have not been chosen for promotion. Try giving yourself a different message. That exam or loss of promotion was an experience from which you can learn; you can look at that one failure as a springboard from which you can bounce back, rather than a steamroller that has flattened your ego.

I find that a number of very sensitive people, especially youngsters, feel that it is difficult to be positive about anything because of the situation of the world as a whole. 'How can we think positively when people are starving in Ethiopia, when people are killing one another, the planet is being polluted, and we are living under the shadow of the bomb?' they ask. They feel they cannot look forward to a future because there may not *be* a future.

I believe that each of us can contribute to the future of the world. Indeed everyone of us is doing so at each moment of the day whether or not we are aware of it. We are not separate from the rest of the world, we are a part of it. We are the trees that make up the forest, and the health of the forest depends upon the health of each individual tree. We can contribute to the peace of the world by learning to experience peace within ourselves. I do not mean that we should close our eyes and escape into meditation but rather that the person who is healthy, happy and clear-minded will have much more to contribute to the peace of the world than people who are bogged down by negative thinking. If each one of us can create more love in ourselves and the environment, then it will be possible for the amount of love in the world to outweigh all the hatred, greed and selfishness that affects so many people's health. But to make that happen, we have to start with ourselves.

Sigmund Freud said many years ago: 'In the final analysis, we must love in order not to fall ill.' This, I am convinced, is a root cause of much of the disease that I treat. What Freud told us all those years ago is now being demonstrated scientifically. Researchers on both sides of the Atlantic are finding that romance is perhaps the best antidote to the common cold. Dr David McCleland, of Boston University, studied one-hundred people, aged eighteen to sixty, to prove the point. He says, 'Dwelling on the positive experiences of loving or being loved appears to raise an individual's concentration of immunoglobulin.' That substance, according to many scientists, is the body's first line of defence against chest infection. Dr McCleland found the substance increased substantially in most people who watched a film about Mother Teresa. Blood samples also showed an increase in T-cells, which combat viruses.

Virologists at Ohio State University found that happily married women have stronger immune systems than women whose marriages have turned sour. Women who have been separated from their husbands for a year or more had less immunity to disease than those who were happily married.

People everywhere are looking for love, feeling sad and rejected when they do not get it. The trouble is that most people are looking for love to come from outside themselves. If as a child you felt loved, you are most likely to feel comfortable expressing your feelings. However, if you felt unloved, you feel threatened and fearful about expressing your innermost feelings, and for protection will bottle them up. Furthermore, if you perceive that one of your parents doesn't love you, in your childlike mind you assume responsibility for this condition by condemning yourself as being unlovable. To compensate for this perceived lack of love, you try to earn love from your parents and peers by pleasing them, a strategy which then gets projected onto all your other relationships. This is why cancer patients, for example, are often 'too good to be true'. Their accommodating, helpful behaviour says, 'Please love and accept me'. Yet our ability to love can only come from within: the best way to put more love into our lives is to start giving love, and the best place to start is by learning to love ourselves.

There is a traditional Buddhist meditation practice often called 'Loving Kindness, Loving Awareness', which I sometimes use during my seminars. Its aim is to experience aspects of love: to love oneself and friends and enemies alike, so creating a global unity. It is a simple exercise which you can easily practise by yourself. Find a comfortable position in which to sit and gently close your eyes.

1. Focus and experience loving yourself. Look at yourself and bring into mind 'Love' and what it means in relation to your own self. Be aware of any associated feelings, impressions, associations, images, or perhaps colours.
2. Focus on love for someone to whom you already feel a close bond. How does love appear in this case? Once more note any associated ideas or feelings.
3. Take as an object of your love a 'neutral' person, someone towards whom you have no particularly strong feelings — someone you feel indifferent to. Once more note any associated ideas or feelings.
4. Now focus on a person you dislike or even feel hatred for; someone who brings about very negative feelings. Extend your love to them.
5. Bring all these together now and extend the *same* feelings of love toward all.
6. The above now moves out to extending love to people in the same room, street, town, country, globally — until the whole earth is surrounded and engulfed by whatever you perceive your own image of love to be.

Many of my patients have had problems during their early years: the death of a parent, a divorce, lack of love or too much criticism from one parent or both. Some people live out their lives looking for the love they did not get as children. Sometimes they also carry around a burden of hatred and resentment towards their parents or the people who have hurt them. It is these feelings which have so often been turned inward against themselves to cause illness. If this is similar to your situation, what can you do about it? Of course, you cannot go back and have your parents do it all over again. What you can do is to start giving *yourself* the love now that you did not receive then. Again, this is something you will need to learn and practise.

   Again, there is a very effective exercise which will help you to release and transmute some of these negative feelings. You will need a partner for this exercise. Sit opposite each other, making direct eye contact, but there should be no verbal communication.

1. Look at your partner and imagine that the other person really likes you. They think you are a nice, kind, loving person and are really happy to be with you. Be aware of any thoughts, feelings symbols, or bodily reactions that occur and examine them.

2. Imagine that your partner really dislikes you. They are criticizing you and looking at you with scorn and hate. Examine what you feel and think now.
3. Imagine your partner is now someone from whom you can learn. See him/her as being an instrument in your growth. Examine how that feels.
4. Imagine the partner to be another soul, a human living being, a fount of unconditional love, someone whom you can accept without condition and vice versa.

At the end of the exercise discuss with your partner your reactions and feelings to each command. Examine, experience and learn from each other how this felt, to be sitting with someone who either loved or disliked you.

It may help if you recognize that a part of you is still an unloved child. Be kind to yourself, as you would be to that child. Encourage and praise yourself, and do not nag yourself if you do not come up to your own expectations. Treat yourself as you would like to have been treated as a child. You can even imagine yourself doing this by seeing yourself as a child and telling that child that *you* love it and want to take care of it.

If you have been through an unhappy or painful childhood or relationship, it does not mean that you have got to be unhappy now. So many people remain locked in the past by continually reliving the events that caused them pain. Tell yourself that your past is not happening to you *now*, unless you are recreating it for yourself. Accept that that is how things happened, and no amount of brooding is going to alter that.

Erin Pizzey, the well-known writer, established a hostel in London for battered wives. She discovered that many of the women who sought refuge after having been beaten up by their spouse or partner had something in common. As children they had been beaten up by their fathers. This again illustrates the way in which people relive the past by projecting it into the present.

If you have suffered a great deal of emotional pain and hurt in the past, you may well be carrying around a heavy burden of anger and resentment against those who hurt you. Sometimes these feelings may have turned into anger and hatred against yourself — self-hatred, for example, is a common cause and symptom of depression. Let it go. Remember that the resentment you feel is producing harmful chemicals in your body and is probably affecting your view of the world as a whole. It will not alter the past one little bit.

Make a decision to release yourself from the past. If you can, forgive the people who have hurt you. They were probably unhappy and confused themselves. By forgiving others, you are helping to heal yourself, and you are also creating space in your life for more positive, helpful people to come in. If the word 'forgive' is difficult for you to accept, then simply think of releasing yourself and breaking the links that tie you to those who hurt you. You can imagine your own pain and anger leaving you like a black cloud and floating away into the distance, getting smaller and smaller until they evaporate into the sky. You can imagine the people you are angry with, and tell them that you forgive them and let them go. Do not imagine yourself hurting them but let them walk away to a distant place where they will be happy and out of your life. You may not initially *feel* forgiving; what is important is your willingness to forgive. You may also need to forgive yourself. Whether you have actually done something that you really regret, and there are very few people who have not, or whether you suffer from that overall sense of guilt that so many people seem to be burdened with, feeling guilty will not put anything right. Remember the child within you who is still growing and learning and is bound to make mistakes. Allow yourself to be imperfect, let the mistakes go, forgive yourself and love yourself.

There is another exercise which looks at ways of dealing with such emotions as fear, anger, jealousy, hurt, sadness, guilt, etc.:

Sit and close your eyes and get in touch with your own body. Now remember a situation in which you felt one of the above emotions (hurt, anger, fear, etc.). Put yourself back into that situation as if it were happening here and now. Recall all the details involved, how you felt, how your body felt etc. Now think of one person you would most like to tell about your emotions but have been unable to. Imagine them there with you — visualize them clearly in every detail. Then imagine talking to this person and being able to freely and openly express whatever it is that you felt. Try to get the feeling you are actually talking directly to this person. Examine how you feel in telling them. How do you see them reacting — is it how you thought they would, or different? Now, however you have seen them reacting, change that to the opposite. Examine the differences you feel in yourself and their changes. Compare the two. Then see yourself telling them with their reacting simply with love, forgiveness, understanding, sympathy — whatever you would most care for in the situation. Hold that image for a while and then release.

Another exercise will help you to learn to love yourself.

Close your eyes and be still. Listen to your breathing. Release the tensions within you as you breathe normally and comfortably. Just let them go on the outgoing breath. Go on to explore your skin. Feel your fingers, the touch of your hand against another part of your body. Become aware of the texture of the floor, chair, your clothing, hair, skin, etc. As you explore yourself and your surroundings, listen to what your body tells you and what images come to mind as you experience the touch and connectedness with all around and within you. Then silently repeat to yourself the following:

'I am in touch with my feelings and being. I love myself for I am a member of the universe. A part of the whole. This is a precious possession. I can love myself. I feel safe, secure and at home within my own body. My body is a safe and pleasurable place to be. Whenever I become anxious or afraid or feel that I am unloved I can relax, breathe and feel safe in my body again. I love myself no matter what. I deserve to be loved, and am loved, and therefore can extend my overwhelming sense of love out to all.'

As you learn to love yourself, you can encourage that loving energy to flow by giving out love. Put love into the things you do during the day. Give out love to a plant or an animal, or to someone that you don't want it back from. Give it out in the form of a smile, or a compliment and remember that as you give a positive stroke to someone else, they are likely to give you one in return. A recently reported study described how elderly people who looked after a dog or a cat were found to have a better record of health and fewer ailments than their counterparts without pets. Clearly this illustrates the point about love. Love is an energy. If you put it out trustingly it will not evaporate, it will come back to you. But remember that if you are weighing up what you are going to get in return, then you are not really giving love at all.

Although I have discussed ways of changing your attitude toward yourself and life, there may be problems in other areas of your life that are affecting your health. Often a patient will be anxious about something but does not know what to do about it or feels frightened of tackling it. This is when worry starts. Worry invariably makes you feel worse and it never solves the problem anyway. So, why worry?

It is important to realize that anxiety itself is not a symptom that there is something wrong with you. It is a signal that something is wrong that you should take some action about. This kind of signal releases hormones that prepare your mind and body for action, and the best way to deal with it is to take action.

There is an old fairy story about a huge monster that lived high in the mountains above a village. It was so gigantic that all the villagers were terrified of it. Occasionally it blew puffs of smoke and flame at them, and when they ran away the monster grew bigger than before.

One day one of the villagers decided to do something about this monster that had been terrifying everyone. He set off up the mountain with a stout stick in search of the monster. Something odd began to happen. The closer he got to the monster, the smaller it became. Until, when he came face to face with it, the monster was only the size of a mouse. Many of our fears are like that. The more we run away from them, the greater they become. If you reverse the process and actually do something about them, you will be putting your attention and energy into what you are doing and the fear and anxiety will diminish.

I suspect that many problems, especially those which affect relationships, are problems of communication. Many people bottle up their problems because they are ashamed of needing help. Human beings are really group animals. We are not meant to cope alone, and there are always people available who are only too glad to help others. I always feel that the best form of help is when the other person enables you to find your *own* answers, rather than telling you what to do. Certainly this is the way in which I prefer to work.

Talking things out with someone else can be helpful in several ways. For example, bringing an anxiety out into the open takes some of the edge off it. Often someone else who is not so close to your problems can see them in a completely different perspective. Talking to someone who accepts you and understands you will also help you feel like the normal, worthwhile person you really are. The knowledge that there is something you can do will help you to regain your self-worth.

No one can wave a magic wand and change you. But once you start letting go of fears and negative thinking about yourself and the world, and putting something more positive in, the clouds *will* start to roll away and you will start the process of self-healing.

4.

Creative visualization

'Creative visualization' is a term that seems often to confuse my patients, usually because they believe that it is something difficult or complicated. You could also call it daydreaming or using your imagination because it's that simple. Everything we do, every action we make, begins as a series of images or pictures in our mind. If you decide to decorate your house, you imagine first of all what it will look like painted in various different colours. If you are asked to direct somebody in a town with which they are not familiar you will be imagining yourself walking or driving down the same streets that you direct them through. Imagery, whose value in healing has been known for thousands of years, is now being woven into the fabric of a wide variety of therapies, and medical uses of imagery are becoming increasingly common.

Everybody visualizes, but in many people, from one-third to one-quarter of the population, the process is subliminal. In other words, their images are so fleeting they are essentially out of the range of awareness. Visualization means bringing into consciousness phenomena that are already occurring and learning to pay attention to them. Often those who have difficulty visualizing are thinking in another sense language: auditory, tactile, or kinesthetic. They may also be expecting too much. Images occur on a continuum from fragments to vivid, Technicolour motion pictures; usually they are less clear than actual perception. If you think you are one of those people who do not easily visualize there are a number of useful exercises which may help you.

The first thing to be aware of is that there is a direct link between relaxation and imagery, and often merely lying down and relaxing is enough to trigger imagery. It is also important to be patient because impatience at having to wait for images to occur can cause a disruptive effect.

Each of us has a preferred sensory mode that we can imagine more easily. Some people can hear music in their minds, others strongly imagine tastes or smells. If you have been vividly imagining a series of flavours, for example lemon, toothpaste or salt, you often find that you slip into a visual image too.

Poor visualizers tend to turn images into words. This transformation happens so quickly that they cannot detect the visual image in the split second before they name it. They act almost like tour guides to their own images but can be helped to visualize by processes that turn off verbal noise. Try looking around you for a few minutes without categorizing, labelling or naming what you see: colours, shapes, or movements. If you slip into naming, just gently return to trying to see without naming.

Another useful exercise is visual recall with a slide projector. Cover the lens of a slide projector with your hand and then remove your hand for a second so you can see the projected image, then cover it again. Try to recall what you saw without naming the object itself — how it *looked*.

Try evoking visual images of something that you really enjoy looking at. Twice a day, for one minute, practice imagining this favourite object, person or place. Try evoking early childhood memories. Remember all you can, clustering recollections of particular times, places, people. Do this twice a day, and after a week review the memories of the previous week. You will find that the earlier the memories, the less dominant is the verbal component.

Drawing your dreams, rather than writing them down, may help you to stay in a visual rather than verbal mode. A final suggestion is learning to picture inner dialogues. When you recognize different aspects of your personality in conflict, try to visualize cartoon characters for them.

I have made all these suggestions to facilitate visualization simply because it forms the cornerstone of all my work and, as you will appreciate during the coming pages, is absolutely crucial in the recovery of my patients. There are basically seven points which I encourage patients to use in their self-healing programme and I will explain each one fully before giving more specific illustrative examples.

1. *Image what your ailment or problem looks like.*
It does not matter if you do not know what a tumour, an arthritic joint, a depression or bad back looks like because my experience is that symbolic, rather than literal, imagery seems to produce better results anyway. Think of your problem and wait for a visual image of it to appear. Verbal language, which can affect overt behaviour, has limitations. The autonomic nervous system, on the other hand, responds to a more basic language — imagery. Conscious expectations about self-healing

can relay information to the autonomic nervous system.

Occasionally I encounter a patient who tells me that they don't want to imagine what their tumour looks like 'because it's giving it more energy'. Typically this is the person who does not want to confront their problem and who believes that by sweeping it under the carpet it will go away. The great majority of those with whom I have worked have found that they feel much more like fighting back against illness once they have a clear image of it.

2. *Imagine any outside treatment you may be receiving attacking the problem and destroying or transmuting it.*
By outside treatment I refer to medical treatment, healing, acupuncture, homeopathy, physiotherapy or any treatment which somebody else is giving you.

3. *Imagine your white blood cells attacking the ailment or problem.*
This is one of the most important points so far as the visualization is concerned. It is your white blood cells which fight off any bodily invader in the form of infection, virus or illness. Your white blood cells form the immune system which is obviously so crucial to the maintenance of health. Visualize the white blood cells as much stronger and much more powerful than the image of the illness. Picture the white blood cells swarming over the deformed cells which are then overpowered and flushed away.

It is essential that your image for the white blood cells is much stronger and more active and, I suggest, aggressive than the illness image. If you find yourself with a strong powerful image for the illness and it is being attacked by one lone white blood cell, your unconscious is almost certainly giving you a message: you have a greater belief in the illness than in the power of your body to recover.

There are two 'schools of thought' so far as visualization is concerned. I encourage my patients to imagine their illness as being rather weak whilst their immune system, their white blood cells, should be visualized as much more powerful and aggressive. I know that quite a number of my patients actually become angry with the illness during their visualization. There is another belief though that one should use much more passive, neutral imagery and that you should avoid aggression or anger creeping into the imagery. After all, it is argued, the illness, whether you like it or not, is a part of you and you should not therefore get angry with yourself. I can only say that from considerable experience and having worked with hundreds of patients, male and female, from different walks of life, the great majority actually feel more comfortable with an aggressive image. They feel that they are really fighting back against something that is basically weak and which they perceive as an ill-advised invader. I have also noticed that the use of aggressive imagery tends to 'exorcise' feelings of anger or resentment which the patient may have been experiencing prior to the onset of disease. Finally, I believe that there may be a danger in using imagery which is too weak or gentle in that it may not have the power to help eradicate the problem. Ultimately though it is up to the patient to decide on a suitable image — aggressive or otherwise.

4. *Imagine yourself as fit and healthy doing all the things you have planned for the future.*
This point may initially seem rather superficial but I believe it is also of crucial importance in a recovery plan. A simple exercise will help you appreciate this.

Sit upright in a comfortable position and, without moving your shoulders, turn your head as far to the left or right as you can. Pick out a spot on the wall which represents as far round as you can see and remember where that spot is. Now turn your head forward again and close your eyes. Imagine now that your neck is made of rubber and that you can turn your head right round through 180 degrees, rather like an owl. Make no physical movements with your head and neck whilst you hold that image in your mind for a minute. Then open your eyes, turn your head in the same direction, and see where the spot goes. Usually you will find that you can turn your head considerably further after visualizing your neck being made of rubber. That is how fast the body responds to visualization. By telling yourself you cannot do something, by imagining the worst, you are giving your body a negative message which it will quickly act upon. By spending a little time each day imagining yourself positively healthy, your body will be accepting that as a message instead.

In 1980 I participated in a pilot study at a well-known hospital, the object being 'to discover what effects, if any, Matthew Manning's healing technique has'. I was asked to treat a number of patients, all of whom were suffering from chronic pain which was not responding to conventional medical treatment. Although I appeared to treat all the patients, I was in reality only properly attempting to heal half of them because, whilst I placed my hands on all of them, with half I was only pretending to heal and was not going through any mental process as I would normally. The object of this deception was to assess whether any benefit that was derived could be accounted for in terms of psychological factors or placebo. If healing were explicable in such terms one would expect all the patients to have benefited, or for those who were helped to be randomly distributed throughout both groups of patients in the study. In fact those patients who had benefited came from the group who had been properly treated. The subsequent report, based on the doctors' evaluation, stated, 'Patients with whom Manning felt he established a good rapport experienced pain relief and/or reduced their drug intake.' The benefits were explained thus: 'The cognitive dissonance theory indicates that, if patients feel involved in any form of treatment, they are more inclined to believe it is working and therefore the more likely it is to work, adding a further dimension to the problem of separating out healing from psychological benefit.'

Although this is a good recommendation for self-healing techniques, it also raises a more disturbing question. If orthodox medicine wants to ascribe healing benefits to healer/patient rapport or 'psychological factors', it should also accept that negative suggestions to patients from their doctors could have a detrimental effect. Dr Brian Roet of the Charing Cross Hospital in London refers to this as 'imprinting': 'Imprinting refers to a direction or command which has been instilled in the back of the mind (out of conscious awareness) and continues to exert its effect year after year,' he says. 'You may think I'm talking about some remote brain-washing science fiction scheme but I can assure you I am not. We have all received imprints at some stage in our life and are carrying them out in one form or another.'

An imprint needs three factors to make it work:

1. a person under stress who is frightened, nervous, and tense;
2. another person of authority with a dominant attitude;
3. a command or prediction made by the authoritarian figure.

In such a situation the command or statement can become imprinted in the back of the mind as an unquestioned command which must be obeyed. This order continues, without the knowledge of the recipient, for years after the initial imprint. Imprints implanted in children by stern parents or school teachers, especially when the child is frightened or guilty and the parent angry. It is as if the words shoot to the back of the mind and lodge there, out of reach of logic. Actions, problems and symptoms which occur later on are not related to the imprinting incidents and failure to change often occurs because of this.

In his book *Anatomy of an Illness*, Norman Cousins, the former editor of the *New York Saturday Review*, describes his successful fight against a crippling rare disease which affected the connective tissues of his body. You will remember from Chapter 2 that he had been given less than a one in 500 chance of recovery by his doctors. He began to mobilize his body's own natural healing resources of laughter, courage and tenacity. The outcome was that he completely recovered. He describes an incident which occurred when he later met the specialist who had given him such narrow chances.

> It was the sheerest of coincidences that, on the tenth anniversary of my 1964 illness, I should happen to meet on the street in New York one of the specialists who had made the melancholy diagnosis of progressive paralysis. He was clearly surprised to see me. I held out my hand. He took it. I didn't hold back on the handshake. I had a point I wanted to make and I thought the best way to do so was through a greeting firm enough to make an impression. I increased the pressure until he winced and asked to be released. He said he could tell from my handshake that he didn't have to ask about my present condition, but he was eager to hear what was behind the recovery.
>
> It all began, I said, when I decided that some experts don't really know enough to make a pronouncement of doom on a human being. And I said I hoped they would be careful about what they said to others; they might be believed and that could be the beginning of the end.

Martin Hitchcock was diagnosed in October 1983 as having cancer of the prostate and bone marrow and became a patient of mine shortly afterwards. In August 1984 he was found to be completely free of the cancer and this has been the case in subsequent six monthly checks. Although his consultant, who had also been treating him with orthodox medical therapies, was described as being delighted with the situation, he warned Martin that the cancer 'could reoccur at any time'.

Gill Hurd came to me with lung cancer early in 1982. She had been advised by her consultant that she had only a limited life expectancy. However, in late 1984, she wrote to tell me that

> my lungs are clear, although my consultant says this is only because the Tamoxifen [a hormonal anti-cancer drug] is having such a dramatic effect on me and that when I become immune to it, 'it' will all come back again. We had a little argument, with me saying I wouldn't let it come back and my consultant saying that although he thought I should continue with what I was doing, nothing would prevent it from returning! My friends and family think that he intended to make me more determined than ever to prove him wrong. I shall certainly endeavour to do so.

Mr D. came to me because he had been told he was terminally ill with cancer of the bowel; when he first came to the Centre he was taking regular doses of morphine every few hours and had a life expectancy of about two weeks. It was August, 1984. From the first healing session he was able to do without morphine. By December he was putting on weight again as he was no longer vomiting. 'I feel healthier and better now than when I was 19,' he told me. Just before Christmas that year he was examined by a doctor and he explained that he had been seeing me. He was told, 'You're only in a temporary remission. You must realize that it won't last.' He died shortly afterwards from a huge tumour which appeared and spread rapidly in his stomach.

Martin Hitchcock, Gill Hurd, and Mr D. could all be claimed to have been given a 'negative placebo'. In my experience this happens quite frequently and, whilst I fully appreciate the paramount need for truth, I think that doctors find themselves too often in a dilemma. Surely my patients could have been told, 'You're in remission at the moment. Let's keep our fingers crossed and hope it lasts.' That is honest and positive. How many people respond to the negative placebo as Gill did? How many more, unaware of the importance of positive attitudes, respond the other way?

5. *Set yourself goals and establish a will to live.*
Goal-setting is a procedure encouraged by the Simontons and is a very good way for the family to band together and assist in the patient's recovery. Setting up goals — three, six and twelve months apart — and keeping the fires burning and optimism alive by reminding the patient, in the bleaker moments, of the goal they have got to reach, is an asset that both family and friends can help with.

Author Cornelius Ryan's 'goal' whilst fighting cancer was to remain alive to write the best-selling *A Bridge Too Far*. He said, 'I can't die with *A Bridge Too Far* unwritten. I can't let cancer kill me until my knowledge of *it* and my work on the new book is done. I have to keep going, even if all the odds are against me. Somehow, someway I will win.' Shortly after the book's completion in November 1973, Ryan said: 'There is a specialness about *Bridge* that cancer made possible. Strange, to say, there is a virtue in having cancer. With the book finished it would be easy to sit back and rest. It would also be dangerous for my morale . . . I feel that inactivity and leisure time would give cancer an edge.'

Another international figure whose 'goal' kept him going is jockey Bob Champion. In 1979, when he was one of the top five jump jockeys in Britain he was diagnosed as having testicular cancer which had spread into the lymph glands in his chest. At the age of 31 he was given eight months to live without treatment. He recounts in his book *Champion's Story* in forthright undramatic terms his feelings and experiences throughout the gruelling two-year period that followed. The initial reaction to the diagnosis left him shocked and scared: '. ... I was petrified. I couldn't understand how I could be ill enough to need an operation when I felt so well. I didn't fancy any doctor operating on my balls. They are a very important part of a man's body.' The fact that he would most probably be left sterile due to the side-effects of the chemotherapy was another cruel blow to Bob who dearly loved children. One overriding thought kept him going through the darkest days of his treatment. He says 'I had an obsession about winning the Grand National on Aldaniti. He made a perfect target for me to regain fitness.' He told his brother-in-law at one point that he would rather be killed in a race than die a lingering death in hospital. His triumph in the 1981 Grand National when he *did* ride Aldaniti to victory is now legend. He said after the race, 'My only wish is that my winning shows there is always hope, and all battles can be won. I just hope it will encourage others to face their illness with fresh spirit.'

I find that not unusually a patient feels trapped or victimized by life; it is important therefore to deal with his problems in a more postiive, creative way. One of the most effective is the setting of new goals which give something to look forward to. These do not necessarily have to be material goals as people so often think.

I knew a man whose wife was seriously ill and hadn't long to live. Knowing that his wife was a great fan of Frank Sinatra he bought in March tickets for a Sinatra concert in London several months later. That gave her a goal because she had always wanted to see Sinatra perform. She survived those months and went to the concert. Her husband kept her going well beyond medical expectation by this system of goal-setting.

As I have already explained earlier in this book, I have frequently observed that the loss of a stabilizing influence in life can contribute to the onset of illness if the patient views their situation as hopeless. Equally it would be true to say that many of these people have lost their goal or role in life. Typically the woman with breast cancer is at an age when her children have recently grown up and left home whilst her husband is at the peak of his career and perhaps spends much time away on business. She then finds that her role as both mother and a wife is unclear. If during childhood she had experienced a lack of closeness with one or both parents, feelings of isolation or neglect could have been caused. As an adult she establishes a strong relationship with someone, but if later in life the relationship is broken up by divorce, death or a child leaving home, this overwhelming loss reconnects her with the childhood feelings. It is as if the later-life incident conclusively reconfirms the hopelessness felt in childhood, a feeling so overpowering that it can bring on cancer.

Viktor Frankel explores the implications and importance of goal establishment in *Man's Search for Meaning*. Frankel, a Jewish doctor imprisoned during World War 2 in a German concentration camp, found that the man who allows himself to decline because he cannot see any future goal is more likely to occupy his mind with retrospective thoughts. There was a tendency to look back to the past and help make the present, with all its atrocities, less real. But in denying the reality of the present there was a danger because it became easy to overlook the opportunities to make something of the camp life. Regarding the present as unreal was an important factor in causing prisoners to lose their hold on life: everything in a way became pointless. The same idea can equally be applied to the patient imprisoned by illness. Many of those with whom I have worked in an effort to alleviate, for example, multiple sclerosis have said that they find it of much greater benefit to concentrate on what they can do than what they cannot do. As Viktor Frankel says,

It is a peculiarity of man that he can only live by looking to the future. And this is his salvation in the most difficult moments of his existence, although he sometimes has to force his mind to the task.

I once had a dramatic demonstration of the close link between the loss of faith in the future and this dangerous giving up. F____, my senior block warden, a fairly well-known composer and librettist, confided in me one day: 'I would like to tell you something, Doctor. I have had a strange dream. A voice told me that I could wish for something, that I should only say what I wanted to know, and all my questions would be answered. What do you think I asked? That I would like to know when the war would be over for me. You know what I mean, Doctor — for me! I wanted to know when we, when our camp, would be liberated and our sufferings come to an end.'

'And when did you have this dream?' I asked.

'In February, 1945,' he answered. It was then the beginning of March.

'What did your dream voice answer?'

Furtively he whispered to me, 'March thirtieth.'

'When F____ told me about his dream, he was still full of hope and convinced that the voice of his dream would be right. But as the promised day drew nearer, the war news which reached our camp made it appear very unlikely that we would be free on the promised date. On March twenty-ninth, F____ suddenly became ill and ran a high temperature. On March thirtieth, the day his prophecy had told him that the war and suffering would be over for him, he became delirious and lost consciousness. On March thirty-first, he was dead. To all outward appearance, he had died of typhus.

Those who know how close the connection is between the state of mind of a man — his courage and hope, or lack of them — and the state of immunity of his body will understand that the sudden loss of hope and courage can have a deadly effect. The ultimate cause of my friend's death was that the expected liberation did not come and he was severely disappointed. This suddenly lowered his body's resistance against the latest typhus infection.

It is vital to have not just one ultimate goal but perhaps a series of goals. The danger in establishing one goal is that when you reach it, you look around and wonder what to do next. I have observed frequently that seriously ill patients will often set themselves a goal of reaching Christmas, perhaps believing it will be their last with their families. Once that goal has been reached, the prospect of another year looms and they now have no goal. The highest mortality rate amongst my patients is during the first two months of a New Year, and I suspect that this Christmas goal-setting is the cause.

A gentleman once had an appointment to see me early one New Year. Shortly before he was due to arrive I received a letter from his partner. 'Gary came out of hospital for Christmas Day, returned on Boxing Day, and then died. Strangely enough he only *believed* he was going to die shortly before Christmas. It seemed he hung on long enough to spend one last Christmas with his family,' he wrote.

It is also apparent that having reasons to live may not be sufficient. Rather, one needs the will to live. Will represents our emotions, and if we find ourselves in a conflict between reason and will our emotions invariably win. The will to live, love of life, positive approach, spiritual calm, mental imagery of recovery and hope, are all keys to the mental complementary approach. In his introduction to the Bristol Cancer Help Centre's booklet on cancer and its non-toxic treatment, Dr Alec Forbes says:

> In my experience, chronic illnesses demand a new set of values: a reassessment at the deepest level of an individual's spiritual, mental and emotional attitudes. I have found again and again that those people who actively change their way of life recover more often than those who drift passively along, taking little or no part in the treatment of their illness . . .

All these points, and many others previously referred to throughout this book, were used by a lady who became something of a legend in the north-west of Britain, Pat Seed. In 1977 she was told that she had cancer and that she had only six months to live by doctors at the Christie Hospital in Manchester where she was being treated. Whilst at the hospital she had walked round the children's ward and had been very touched by the fact that the children there would never know the joy that she had had in life with her husband and own children. She then found that the hospital was without a scanner and that the National Health Service did not have sufficient funds to be able to pay for one. She decided that, if it was the last thing she did, she would raise the money to buy one. At the time she did not realize that they cost £1 million each.

Nine months later, having embarked upon her fund-raising campaign, it dawned on her that she was not supposed to be still alive. The outcome was that Pat Seed went on to raise £4 million and was awarded an MBE for her efforts. Ironically the campaign provided the kind of cure that all the medicine and technology in the world could not achieve. She beat the cancer.

In 1983, Dr Brian Eddlestone, head of diagnostic radiology at the Christie Hospital, admitted

> But for her committment to this campaign it is very doubtful Pat would still be here today. That she is alive defies medical explanation. When she came here there was no treatment we could offer that would have prolonged her life for six years. I believe she has survived cancer because she decided she desperately wanted to live, that she had something great to do and that, having started it, she wanted to see it through to the end.
>
> It would be wrong for me, as a doctor, to suggest a bit of fighting spirit can beat cancer but against this is the fact that every now and again we get a patient who appears to do just that. Pat is an inspiration to us all.

Pat Seed herself explained,

> One day I suddenly realized I'd lived three months more than I was supposed to — I'd been so busy I hadn't even had time to think about dying. I can see now that by finding a cause and becoming completely immersed in it, I was fighting, by not letting it get me down. It's all a question of attitude. I heard about two cancer patients who, like me, were given six months to live.
>
> One went home, made arrangements for his funeral and died a fortnight later. The other went home, looked at his seven children and thought, 'How on earth will this lot cope if I go?' Now, 20 years later, those children have grown up and he's still alive. My philosophy all along has been to take one day at a time. When cancer patients ring me for advice I always hope I can inspire them to have a fighting spirit.

She went on to say that the most important to her had been the love and support of her husband Geoff. 'He's been the rock upon which

I've leaned, and the one person to whom I could tell every waking thought.'

Tragically Geoff Seed was killed in an explosion at a water-pumping station at Abbeystead in Lancashire in 1984. Months later Pat Seed died too, of kidney failure.

Pat Seed should be an example to everyone because she demonstrated so dramatically that you can beat the odds. Her story illustrates powerfully that if you have a goal you can keep going. Her comment about her husband, who obviously had been a tower of strength, echoes what I wrote early in the book.

It could be said that her advice to take one day at a time does not sit easily with the concept of goal achievement. However, Pat Seed patently had a goal and still took one day at a time. She lived in the present and, as Victor Franke says, it is essential to do this rather than become retrospective.

6. *Think and act positively. Learn to love and forgive.*
Several studies have shown that the cancer-prone person, besides feeling abandoned, also suffers from low self-esteem and an inability to express negative feelings. As I explained in Chapter 2, many of my patients have a poor self-image and I made numerous suggestions to help nurture love and forgiveness. Although it is somewhat of a generalization, I suspect that cancer patients tend to bottle up their feelings.

Quite often when a patient comes with their partner to the Centre for the first time it is the partner rather than the patient who does much of the talking. Rather like a ventriloquist act, if I ask the patient a question, the partner will answer on their behalf. 'It's so unfair,' they will tell me. 'My husband's been such a good man all his life. He's been on school committees, he's raised money for chairity, he's always the perfect gentleman — helping old ladies across the road. And, do you know, I've never seen him get cross or lose his temper in all those years?'

The wife has told me much more than she realizes. Her husband is one of those people who does not let others know that he is angry, sad or hurt; often the world regards them as saint-like figures. They are long-suffering and almost too good to be true. Ironically, though, that benign goodness actually indicates how little faith they have in expressing themselves.

If as a child you feel loved, you are most likely to feel comfortable in expressing your feelings. If, however, you feel unloved, you may feel threatened and frightened about expressing your deepest feelings and, for protection, you bottle them up. Furthermore, if you feel that one of your parents, or your wife or husband, does not love you, you take responsibility for this in your own mind by condemning yourself as being unlovable. As we have said before, to compensate for this perceived lack of love, you try to earn love from those around you by pleasing them. Consequently cancer patients are often 'too good to be true'. Their helpful and self-effacing behaviour is saying, 'Please love and accept me'.

I believe that forgiveness is crucial to the healing process. If you have been involved in a broken relationship and you are holding feelings of anger, resentment or bitterness, you are harming only yourself. Those feelings do not have any effect on the other party. Resentment effectively says that you refuse to take responsibility for the love and nurturance that you are no longer receiving.

One simple but effective exercise to help you to love and release can be practiced during a few quiet moments at the end of the day. Think first of three things for which you are grateful; then think of three things that you forgive or release; finally, think of three things that you would like to have happen in your life.

7. *Give yourself a mental pat on the back.*
This reinforces the fact that *you* are doing something to help yourself.

Having now listed and described each of the seven points that I use with my patients in their self-healing programme, you will be aware that they may not all be relevant to your particular situation. It is a matter of choosing those points which are helpful and then working with them. .

So far as the visualization is concerned there are some important points to consider. There is also certainly a right and a wrong way to visualize. I have often found that children are much better at using imagery than adults, which is probably because children tend to have greater imaginations than adults and they have not been so extensively trained to think rationally, analytically, or logically. I once treated a small girl who had tumours on various nerve endings throughout her body. I remember explaining to the girl's mother about visualization whilst the mother looked at me in disbelief as if to say, 'How do you expect my little girl to understand something like this?' I then turned and explained it as simply as I could to the child herself. She understood it almost immediately. When she returned some weeks later she told me what she had been imagining.

Her tumours were represented by slices of cheese and her white blood cells by white mice. Several times each day the mice would appear and nibble away at the slices of cheese. If she was still in pain she would occasionally try to visualize the white mice getting on to her father's motorbike so that they could travel from one slice of cheese to the next more quickly. That kind of imagery was perfect because the tumours were represented by something that could not fight back and the immune system was symbolized by mice which could rapidly eat away at the tumour. Subsequently adult patients have used similar imagery and have found white mice or rats doubly effective because they so quickly breed and multiply. Symbolically this would of course represent a strengthening of the immune system.

More recently I have been treating a boy of six who is suffering from diabetes. This means that his pancreas is not producing sufficient insulin. This may not be the easiest thing to visualize when one first thinks about it. However, the young boy concerned came up with a marvellous image in which his pancreas was represented by a factory that pressed oranges to produce juice or insulin. Unfortunately all the workers in the factory were were lazy and sat around having tea-breaks which meant that juice production was less than it could be. During his visualization sessions he imagined these workers starting to press more oranges in a bid to increase productivity so that his insulin level was increased.

Both of these examples are excellent but there is also another way in which images may occur which, although giving clear messages about how you really feel about getting well again, simply will not work.

Some years ago I worked with a middle-aged man who had come for healing with a very large tumour in his chest. As soon as he met me for the first time he told me how helpful he had found my cassettes and that he had been listening to them regularly. I asked him to tell me what he had been visualizing.

His tumour, he said, was represented by an iceberg and his body's defences were represented by himself standing astride the iceberg wielding a pick axe with which he was attempting to break up the mass of ice. That image was useless because there was no way that he was going to single-handedly destroy that iceberg. It did, however, give a clear insight into what he really, perhaps unconsciously, believed about his illness: he was prepared to make a token effort but he knew that he would not succeed. I explained why this imagery was not suitable and the following week he returned again. This time his tumour was represented by a tree stump that had roots spreading into his chest. His white blood cells were symbolized by snow flakes and several times each day he was visualizing a blizzard which completely covered the tree stump. Again, this was of no benefit at all because the problem was merely being covered up rather than destroyed or transmuted. He died not long afterwards and I think he knew that he was dying and that this influenced his imagery. On numerous subsequent occasions

I have found that at a certain point a patient will either stop visualizing or, in spite of their apparent efforts, images fail to occur; invariably the patient dies not long afterwards. Dennis Jaffe, director of the Family Health Clinic in Los Angeles, helps patients to use imagery to gather information about their illnesses. These images, he says, carry potential meaning, sometimes suggesting significance in the type of illness an individual has. Jaffe urges his patients to engage in a dialogue with such images so that they discover they have the power to learn from and change their symptoms.

Although I am always happy to suggest visual images to my patients, I prefer them to first make an attempt to arrive at their own images. It is not a matter of concentration, of holding your breath, or of knitting your brows. Instead it is a process of relaxation and 'letting go'. Usually those patients who experience difficulty with visualization will concentrate on producing imagery for two or three weeks, becoming increasingly impatient because nothing is happening. Just at the moment that they decide it will not work for them, the images will occur quite spontaneously simply because they have ceased concentrating. I prefer them to go through this process rather than taking the easy step of suggesting an image because an image which represents strength and determination to me may well represent, say, anger and resentment to someone else. Furthermore, by arriving at your own image you are invoking your own creative energies which will assist you in your recovery. The suggestions for imagery which I will make here should therefore be regarded as illustrative examples to be used only if necessary!

The majority of my cancer patients seem to use imagery which in some way involves water. Typically they will visualize the cancer cells as being weak, confused and undirectional grey fish. (There is a tendency to imagine cancer cells as black in colour which I would discourage because of the negative emotional connotations of that colour.) These disorganized and weak fish are then eaten by shoals of piranha fish or sharks which symbolize the white blood cells. If they are also receiving, for example, chemotherapy, they will work to incorporate this into the imagery by visualizing that a tanker with a cargo of barrels of toxins has passed overhead. As it did so, one of the barrels broke free and burst open in the water. The poisons have drifted through the water killing off the small grey fish whilst the large strong predators are unaffected.

I once gave healing to a man suffering from a form of leukaemia in which he had far too many white blood cells and insufficient red cells. This obviously caused some confusion since one should normally visualize powerful white blood cells. One evening, after several days of trying to arrive at an effective visualization without success, he was watching a Western on television. That gave him the idea for the imagery that he then used. His white blood cells were symbolized by cowboys whilst the red cells became Red Indians. During his visualization sessions he imagined the two sides fighting one another but it was always the cowboys who were injured and killed and the Indians who became the victors. He then began a course of chemotherapy which he took in the form of tablets; this became incorporated into the imagery in the form of crates of weapons and ammunition which the Red Indians always got hold of and used against the cowboys to kill off even more of them. Within a matter of weeks his blood cell count began to stabilize in a way that it had not done for eighteen months previously.

Of course, visualization does not work only on cancer. I have produced a wide range of cassettes which deal with a variety of problems that respond positively to the techniques of relaxation and visualization: osteoarthritis, allergies, high blood pressure, pain, phobias, etc.

Most hypertensives, or people suffering from high blood pressure, bear deeply repressed anger, resentment or fear but hide inner hostility with an outer display of restraint and nonchalance. The resulting inner conflict reinforces stress and sends blood pressure soaring. Studies conducted in Europe and the USA show that there is an above average incidence of high blood pressure in people whose jobs entail high levels of responsibility. There is a wealth of evidence to demonstrate that high blood pressure can be reduced by relaxation alone but less to show that the addition of visualization brings about an even more marked reduction. Dr Kenneth Pope of the Brentwood Veterans Administration Hospital in California taught a group of hypertensive patients to imagine their blood vessels increasing in diameter whilst in a state of relaxation. (As your blood pressure rises, you blood vessels become compressed by the pressure.) He found that it helped to lower their blood pressure much more effectively than another group of patients who were using only relaxation.

Many patients suffering from allergies have experienced considerable relief from visualization. Although there is no firm consensus of opinion as to what actually happens to cause an allergic reaction, the general belief is that up to one-third of the population are born with a predisposition to allergies although far fewer actually go on to manifest them. It seems that periods of exceptional stress can often precipitate their onset. The immune system then goes haywire and, instead of fighting off bacteria, germs, infections, viruses and so on, starts to fight itself when certain substances, or allergens, are introduced to the system. Let us take the example of somebody who is allergic to bread.

Imagine your white blood cells as an army of infantrymen and, as you imagine yourself eating a slice of bread, visualize the soldiers suddenly going into mutiny as they attack one another. Very quickly powerful generals and officers arrive, charging in on huge powerful white horses. They shoot into the air and shout at the infantrymen to fall back into rank. Obeying the instructions of these officers, symbolically representing a form of 'super' immune system, they become peaceful again. Then imagine yourself once more eating the slice of bread whilst the officers look on. This time all the soldiers behave and there is no rebellious behaviour. When you have practiced this form of visualization for two or three weeks, actually eat some bread whilst imaging. This imagery has certainly been successful not just for those with one or two minor allergies but also for a number of people suffering from more serious multiple allergies.

A similar form of imagery can be used to help overcome phobias. Let us take the example of an agoraphobic person who has difficulty in visiting shops. Whilst sitting in a relaxed state, think of something that you would like to buy from a shop that you already know. Maybe you want to buy a book. Imagine yourself calmly putting on your coat and walking out of the front door. See yourself taking a deep breath as you leave your house and visualize yourself walking down the street or through the town to the bookshop. If at any point you feel yourself becoming tense, make a conscious effort to relax by breathing deeply and reminding yourself that you are only imagining it — you are not actually going through the action physically. Imagine yourself, still remaining calm, walking into the bookshop and gently browsing through the shelves until you find the book you have been looking for. You pick up the book and take it to the cashier, pay for it, smile at the cashier, and leave the shop. Visualize yourself remaining relaxed and calm; focus on your breathing and imagine making the return journey home with the book. When you have practised this several times over the period of one or two weeks actually make that journey that has thus far been only in your mind. If at any point you feel yourself getting tense, just remember the simple relaxation technique of breathing deeply. Once you have successfully reached the shop once, the phobia will in all likelihood have been dispelled for good.

I have also found that various arthritic conditions respond favourably to visualization; at the very least it seems that inflammation and pain are frequently reduced even if greater mobility in joints is not necessarily experienced. Of over 200 different forms of arthritis, osteoarthritis is the most prevalent. The cause of this form of arthritis is usually wear and tear on joints which produces an erosion of the cartilage. This in turn produces inflammation and, as the bones start to rub against one another without the protection of the cartilage, deposits of calcium accumulate. For visualization one can use very much the same kind of image as for cancer: imagine, for example, the calcium deposits as crystals of ice and that the white blood cells are represented symbolically by men carrying blow torches to melt away the icy deposits.

In treating hundreds of patients I have always felt that quality of life is the most important consideration. Certainly I now believe that quality of life is more important ultimately than quantity. One of the greatest detractions from this quality of life is pain. I feel that if I can do no more for somebody than relieve pain, I have achieved something. You can live with arthritic joints or a weak back far more easily if you are pain free. There is a close connection between pain and tension. If, for example, you have a nerve pinched between two vertebrae in your spine, all the muscles in that area will go into spasm to protect the nerve from being further damaged. Although the body succeeds in this aim the other consequence is that the tension actually prevents the vertebrae and discs from returning to their correct positions which means that the pain is maintained. Pain invariably causes tension and tension invariably worsens pain. Simple relaxation is therefore one of the most effective pain controllers. Two visualization techniques have proved very helpful on numerous occasions.

The first is relatively simple. Imagine that you are walking through a beautiful garden filled with flowers and wonderful exotic plants. Coursing through this garden is a sparkling bubbling stream which cascades cool water over polished stones. Imagine that you sit by the edge of this stream and allow your feet to dangle in the water. See the pain being washed out of your body through your feet and imagine it flowing downstream, just as mud from a dirty pebble would be carried downstream.

The second visualization technique is remarkably effective although I do not claim to know why. It was developed by Norman Shealy, Associate Professor of Neurosurgery at the Universities of Wisconsin and Minnesota and Director of the well-known Pain Rehabilitation Centre in La Crosse, Wisconsin, USA. Imagine first of all what the pain looks like. Imagine the size, shape and colour — very often pain will appear as a red, pulsing ball. Then imagine that you are removing the pain from your body and that it is suspended in the air a few feet in front of you. Allow it now to expand and grow to whatever size it chooses; if in your body it seemed the size of a grapefruit, it may enlarge to the size of a football that is red and glowing. Visualize that red ball losing its intensity of colour and becoming pink rather than red before it begins to reduce in size. Allow it now to reduce to whatever dimension it chooses. It may return to its original size or become the size of, say, a table tennis ball. Imagine now that its pink colour begins to fade away and that it becomes instead a relaxing, cool, pale green ball. When you have imagined it thus for a while, visualize yourself putting this green ball back into the same area of your body that the red ball was originally taken from. This may not bring about permanent pain relief but it certainly seems effective in the shorter term. I can only assume that the reason for this lies in the connection between our emotional responses to different colours.

One of the most effective forms of pain control that I am aware of does not use visualization and could be called 'substituting pleasure for pain'. Although it sounds unlikely, it works well. I once treated a lady who some years earlier had been involved in a motor accident and had received severe spinal injuries which left her with constant and almost intolerable pain in her back and legs. She had been virtually housebound for seven years, fearful that if she went out the pain would intensify and she would seize up. After several healing sessions with me her pain level had dropped considerably, even though it was still present, and after a few more treatments it was obvious that I was having no further beneficial effect on it. I then began to suspect that she had become accustomed to living with the pain and that she was suffering more from fear of pain than real pain.

I suggested to her husband that he take her out shopping one day, something she had not done for years since her accident. Throwing up her hands in horror she exclaimed that she could not possibly do something like that. Later that week, however, her husband took up my suggestion and on a Saturday morning took her shopping in a local town. For almost three hours she was apparently pain free, something she had not experienced for seven years. It was not necessarily that her pain had left but rather that for those three hours her attention had been diverted away from herself and her back towards everything around her. The irony is that many people who suffer regularly from chronic pain become housebound by choice with the consequence that they are continually monitoring themselves and asking whether the pain is better or worse than it was half an hour ago.

The case that I have cited is really not that unusual. People will often overcome great obstacles if their attention is diverted away from themselves. Terrie Hayes is a teenager from South Yorkshire who has had both her legs amputated below the knee. Having won a bravery award in the Barnardo's Champion Children of the Year she was due to collect an award from Princess Diana. For three days before the award giving ceremony Terrie had been off school because of the pain in her legs. On the big day things were different. 'I can't remember a thing we talked about but speaking to the Princess made me forget the pain,' she said. 'Nothing was going to stop me coming here today to meet the Princess.'

Of course, when we are tired, tense, depressed or unwell, we feel pain much more than we do if we are caught up in the excitement of a situation.

Sportsmen and women will sometimes suffer quite serious injury of which they are quite unaware until their event has finished.

Probably the most common cause of pain is 'the bad back'. I was told a fascinating and amusing story by a lady who attended a seminar I once presented. She had suffered from a slipped disc which is one problem almost guaranteed to cause acute pain. She had been advised to lie for a couple of weeks on a hard surface or on the floor; she knew that this was one of the few orthodox solutions to her problem because she was herself a practising physiotherapist. She had been therefore lying very still on the floor waiting for Nature to take its course when it occurred to her that visualization might help her to recover more quickly. As she relaxed and began to imagine her spine, a clear and anatomically precise picture began to form in her mind's eye. She then perceived one disc which was out of alignment with the others and pressing on a nerve. She was wondering what image she could possbily use to ease the slipped disc back into place when something happened that she was not expecting and had not consciously instigated. It was so ridiculous it made her laugh. For coming down her spine was the Tetley tea-bag man, who appears in television commercials, pulling a garden roller behind him! When he came to the damaged area he very carefully rolled the spine until the offending disc was 'pushed' back into place again. Within a matter of days she was up on her feet again and back at work, pain free. I think that this example is of particular interest because it shows that the unconscious mind will come up with images for visualization if you allow them to flow. It is not so much a matter of *thinking* of an image, but of allowing one to form spontaneously.

There was an interesting follow-up to this story. The physiotherapist was sufficiently impressed by her experience to encourage her patients to use visualization techniques whilst she worked on them. She discovered that those who visualized during physiotherapy treatment responded much more quickly and positively than those who declined to do so.

A common misconception about healing, and indeed about many

other complementary therapies, is that the patient must relinquish medical treatment. My own view is that no one therapy has all the answers and I feel that the patient has the greatest opportunity for recovery when using several therapies, perhaps orthodox and unorthodox, together. Unfortunately it is this misconception which has given complementary therapies a rather tarnished image in the eyes of some of the medical profession. I make no attempt to persuade my patients in any direction so far as treatment is concerned, but I often treat people who have declined medical treatment because of its possible side-effects, its impingement upon quality of life, or because of simple fear. A large proportion of my cancer patients tend to be reticent about agreeing to radiation therapy or chemotherapy because of the possible side-effects which will often include vomiting or nausea and loss of hair. However, I have found on repeated occasions that healing and self-healing techniques will reduce and possibly even eliminate these unpleasant side-effects.

Expectation of negative side-effects seems to be a significant factor in the patient's subsequent reaction. Those who expect the worst and who anticipate nausea, discomfort and loss of hair are more likely to experience these things than those who approach the treatment more open-mindedly. If you can imagine the chemotherapy, or whatever medical treatment you may be receiving for whatever problem, as something which is actually helping you, your subsequent response is likely to be much better. Two cases in which I have been involved are of particular interest.

The first involves a young man, Andrew Burn, who had cancer which was treated also by chemotherapy and radiotherapy. His chemotherapy was administered intravenously and he was warned that the treatment, which was being repeated every three weeks for six months, would cause him to be sick and to lose his hair. He was told that he would just start to be feeling better after the last bout of chemotherapy when the next one would come up. Whilst receiving the chemotherapy he tried his best, in what must have been hardly ideal circumstances, to imagine the drugs in the chemotherapy killing off his cancer cells. He also imagined himself being completely fit and playing golf. Although he lost his hair, the nausea and vomiting seemed to be substantially less than he had been led to expect and usually he *was* out playing golf forty-eight hours later.

The second involves a lady whom I will refer to as Joan. She had cancer of the bones and was also receiving chemotherapy and had also been given the same warnings. She was not at all happy with the prospect of losing her hair which she took a great deal of time in looking after. During the time of her treatment she visualized her hair as coconut matting, imagining that all her hairs were knotted underneath her scalp to prevent them from falling out. Her hair remained in place!

One of the greatest proponents of self-healing is an American radiation oncologist, Dr Carl Simonton, the founder of the Cancer Counselling and Research Centre in Fort Worth, Texas. He became interested in the role of mind over body because of his observations of women who he was treating with radiation therapy. He noticed that those who anticipated the worst experienced the most severe side-effects. A massive dose of radiation would cause no side-effect in one patient, whereas a very small dose would cause a considerable side-effect in another patient. He then discovered that Japanese women tended to respond much more badly, which he assumed was due to the inherent fear of radiation within most Japanese after the dropping of the atomic bombs in World War 2.

In a broader sense many of these ideas are now being incorporated into orthodox medical treatment. Anaesthetists, for example, are teaching relaxation techniques to patients who are about to undergo surgery, so that they will feel less pain afterwards. Hospital staff have also found that patients who can relax require fewer pain-killing drugs.

One of the major cancer research organizations recently began funding an experiment due to run over several years aimed at assessing the true value of visualization. A large number of women with breast cancer are being monitored, and, although all of them are receiving orthodox medical treatment, half are being asked to use relaxation and visualization as well to determine the benefits.

I am sure that if they find nothing else, they will soon discover that, through these techniques, the patient begins to activate his motivation to be well and to arouse emotions and problems into consciousness where they can be dealt with.

5.

The spiritual aspects of illness

Carved over the portals of an ancient Greek temple can be found the Delphic precept translated as 'Man know thyself and Thou shalt know the Universe'. But how many of us can say that we truly 'know ourselves'? The German poet, scholar, statesman and author of the legendary *Faust*, Johann Wolfgang von Goethe, shed some light on this question when he said '"Know thyself"? If I knew myself, I'd run away'. As a rule, we are often afraid to delve too deeply into our psyche; scared perhaps that in so doing the inner growth work may open up a Pandora's box of unresolved devils and demons (fears, insecurities, hurts, pains and the like).

We often hear that a person dealing with serious illness can aid a return to health in an effective and positive way by developing an outside support system, such as family, friends, support groups, etc. I feel that whether one is presently in good health or not, that we also need to develop an *inner support system*. The baiss for this will stem naturally from first of all looking closely at our attitudes, emotions, feelings, responses and relationships; detaching ourselves from those that hold us back, generate bad feelings, or in some way prohibit us from acting more fully and freely. Then changing what we *can* change, and releasing that which we *cannot* (or do not need) by opening up our hearts to unconditional love and forgiveness; and developing our awareness and capacity to feel and think and know and grow and operate within our bodies more lovingly and more effectively.

Our sum total as a human living, thinking, breathing individual has been shaped by events, people and experiences in our past: parents, friends, religion, school, health, environment, work, hobbies, relationships, and many other factors. While it is nice to hold memories of happy and enjoyable events from the past, we also, unfortunately, harbour as many — if not more — negative ones as well. You cannot change what has already happened, yet how often do we go back in our mind over and over a past event: worrying over or regretting a word or deed, and wondering how we could have changed things. Why bother worrying and getting upset and stressed over things you are powerless to alter at this stage? You have the power to free yourself from being a victim of your past. You, and you alone, are the only one who can make that change. Books, therapies and philosophies can assist and guide, but they really cannot do the inner work for you. Until we really *know ourselves*, how can we begin to know, understand, and be of assistance to *others*?

So, how do we go about embarking on this 'inner journey' to understand ourselves? I don't have the ultimate steadfast answer to that question — and I doubt anyone else does either. I can offer you ways and ideas, but the process is unique to each individual, and that is where the decision lies in choosing the right path to take. Without doubt the most important work you can ever do is upon yourself. Confronting and understanding your fears, instead of opting for visible alternatives is a pre-requisite to your own personal growth work. Life is change — a continual ever-changing process — and trying to halt that change and personal inner growth is a way of denying that process; trying to change others to induce *them* to remain static in order that you can keep the illusion of remaining the same, wastes valuable energy that could be channelled elsewhere to better use.

Why use up so much time and effort on a futile cause when you could utilize it so much more effectively in going with the ebb and flow of life and enjoying your unfolding potential? It is also a process that takes time, just as profound changes that occur in our lives do not happen overnight. We may feel one day we have taken two steps forward — to go one step back the following day. This is all part of life's rich experience, and the aim should be to direct this towards strengthening the potential within ourselves to grow: to develop greater harmony and expression.

The first step on our growth path must, without question, be to relax more. Every day of our lives we encounter major and minor stressors of one kind or another. It may be a relatively minor thing, such as oversleeping and having to dash to catch the train to work. From the minute you opened your eyes and saw the time, you began scurrying frantically around like the White Rabbit from *Alice In Wonderland* muttering 'I'm late! I'm late!' By the time you have actually caught the train (with literally seconds to spare), you flop down exhausted in your seat, with heart pounding madly and perspiration dotting your brow. Or the stressor could be of a more serious nature, such as perhaps being fired from your job, or having a minor car accident. Relaxing means not only putting your body at rest, but also relaxing your mind *and* whole approach to life in general. It is an important step in self-improvement and in developing awareness.

To begin, start to put into practice the four methods of relaxation I outlined in Chapter 2: mental imagery, breathing, exercise, laughter. And don't forget meditation, a vital component in relaxed living.

The more you are able to relax, the more effective you will become in whatever it is you seek to achieve. Getting caught up in life's traps is very easy. By relaxing you will be able to think more clearly, and thereby avoid many of the obstacles that lay in your path. As you become more centred you will go with the flow of the river of life rather than be forever fighting against it. You will become more aware of the currents of life (your own responsibilities, limitations, interests and concerns, and those of others) and ride with them as you 'be' rather than 'do'. Stop searching for love, happiness, health, prosperity — start BEING happy, healthy, prosperous, loving — and — loved.

In today's society we do not project our natural spirituality. We are far from expressing the true essence of our being, the loving and beautiful sides of our nature, either because life itself does not often appear to allow it, or our finer sensitivities become submerged by values such as money, power, prestige, etc., all the while drawing us further away from our inner self.

We tend to look to the various complementary therapies and self-healing techniques only when we happen to fall ill. I feel that gradually people are becoming aware that we need to move away from healing only once sickness has established itself and, instead, put the emphasis on using healing as a means to becoming more of a complete, whole person BEFORE illness has an opportunity to take hold; and when it does, be better equipped psychologically to deal with it. Slowly we are seeing changes in the way we think about ourselves, our bodies, our health, our minds. The growth of seminars on increasing personal knowledge, awareness and self-realization, reflects this changing outlook. People are now saying: 'I want to know more about who I am;' 'I want to explore and get in touch with my inner self;' 'I want to participate in my health recovery programme and be responsible for my own well-being.'

One means of relaxation I have not so far mentioned is music. Music is unique and powerful in its influence; a communication that is more often than not a *non-verbal* communication: it is the *wordless* meaning of music that gives it its potency and value — the common denominator that transcends boundaries between cultures, races and tongues.

Music as a definite healing force is not something to have become known over recent years — it's inception came thousands of years ago, and down through history and from many different parts of the world has come concrete proof of music as a therapeutic force in health and healing. It evokes a healing energy probably through its ability to soothe the mind and induce a meditative state in the listener that relaxes the left hemisphere of the brain while at the same time stimulating the right. Music is able to produce a mood, or intensify an existing one, in every listener. Psychiatrists have found that music has the power to change one mood into another, and is capable of replacing states of grief, depression, despair and hopelessness. In physiological experiments music has been shown to have the exact opposite effect on the body to anger — one of the most destructive emotions, arising out of dissatisfaction, unhappiness, unfulfillment or discouragement. Anger increases the pulse rate, raises the blood pressure, interrupts the flow of gastric juices, interferes with digestion and causes tension in the muscles. Conversely, music slows the pulse rate, lowers blood pressure, restores the flow of gastric juices to the stomach, aids the digestive processes, and has an overall relaxing effect on the body.

Pythagoras, the Greek physician, philosopher, mathematician and astronomer, set up an academy at Crotona in 539BC where his students followed a curriculum that included meditation, dance, correct diet, mathematics, astronomy, and, music; believing that the harmony achieved through the combination of music, dance and numbers was vital to the health of mind and body.

It has only been over the last 30 years or so that music therapy has been put into regular practice and extensively tested for therapeutic value. A hospital in Montreal used classical music successfully as a painkiller. In Poland a study conducted of over 400 sufferers of various types of neurological disease and severe headaches, showed that after six months those who listened to music had been able to greatly reduce the number of drugs taken. Those who had not had the benefit of music showed no change. In the delivery room at the University of Kansas Medical Center, painkilling drugs were used with less frequency and labours made easier and faster when music was played in the background.

I use music extensively in the course of my work, and have produced a range of tapes by artistes whose music I regularly use and can personally recommend for its soothing and relaxing quality, and effectiveness in visualization and self-healing. Among these are: The Enid — *Inner Pieces, Inner Visions*; Paul Fitzgerald and Mark Flanagan — *Quiet Water*; Annie Locke — *The Living Earth, Portraits*; Mike Rowland — *Solace, The Fairy Ring, Silver Wings*.

Music helps us to focus and strengthen our capacity to feel, encourages vivid imagery, and releases our inner anxieties. Try the following exercise to bring you in touch with the power of music and its effect on the senses.

Select a piece of music (the choice is yours — whatever you feel most comfortable with, be it classical, folk, pop, New Age or other) and settle yourself down in a comfortable place where you feel relaxed and will not be interrupted. Turn up the volume to a level which feels right and is loud enough to shut out any outside noises (ticking of a clock, street sounds, etc.). Lay down on the floor with your arms placed at either side of your body, palms down on the floor. Let the music flow over you. Feel as it reverberates in, over, and around your entire body. Let yourself become part of the music. If you feel uneasy or faint, just concentrate on breathing deeply for a few seconds and the sensation will pass; you can then begin to trust yourself to go with the sounds and energies you are feeling throughout your body. Whatever thoughts or images come into your mind, just notice what you are experiencing, and then let them drift away on the music. Stay with this happy relaxed state for 20-30 minutes: at one with sound; freeing yourself from your daily stresses, worries, health/money/relationship problems. Listen to what the music says to you as it washes completely over your body like a soothing wave, taking with it all that you have been suppressing within your mind and body.

The feelings that make us feel uncomfortable (such as fear, guilt, anger, greed, and jealousy) offer us the opportunity to move forward through exploration and growth. Yet how often do we attempt to smother and damp them down when they arise from our innermost depths, saying, for example: 'I feel sad' — and then quickly going on to 'I want to be happier', without questioning the reason underneath which has caused our sadness in the first place. This can be equated with orthodox medicine providing a pill or potion to treat a symptom — yet leaving the causative factor untreated. I feel — and since I began introducing a section in my workshops on exploring and releasing our negativities early in 1987, it has become more apparent — that the way ahead lies in looking closely at our discomfort; facing ourselves, our feelings and our emotions, openly and honestly and really listening to what we are telling ourselves. Instead of trying to ignore these unsettling feelings, we should be looking upon them as guides to where we limit our awareness.

There are ways in which you can focus on these feelings, and in so doing, explore and learn from them. They can be pointers to help you identify where you have been blocking, and to enable you to welcome your feelings during the process of exploration; allowing yourself to be who you are and to release those stifled energies within.

Keeping a diary or some form of record, either in book form or on tape, is a good place to begin to focus on and note the unfolding of our thoughts as they occur. You do not have to be a prodigious writer and it doesn't matter if you have difficulty with grammar, since the only eyes to see it will be yours. How you express yourself is up to you — there is no right or wrong way. Perhaps to begin you may like just to sit with your eyes closed and cast your thoughts back over the day: the events, the people, the places, the situations. Watch what passes through and, after reflecting on these, write down what seems to you to have taken priority. Allow your innermost feelings to be aired in whatever way seems most natural and easy. Focus on any meetings with others — did you feel uncomfortable with them? or at ease? What feelings did they generate in you during the encounter — tenseness? anger? hurt? joy? love? If you encounter a block in being able to write, just sit for a while and reflect on where the reluctance is coming from, or you can simply write down that you feel unable to express what has happened in words. You can always return to it later when your insight may be clearer.

You can now go on to exploring a situation, relationship, or feeling, by looking at the following points:

Your expectations: What you feel you sometimes *have* to do, what you blame yourself for having done or not done.

Your fears: Let this open to its full extent. Explore the fear: what might happen, what others may think of you, what would be the worst thing that could happen, what would be the result. Writing these down and viewing them can help with an objective view to what you could do to change these fears. Are they really necessary after all? You may find that their power will have decreased.

Your past experiences: These are very often connected with present feelings and need letting out. Look at how something in the past is perhaps the underlying cause for your present feeling. Examine the attitudes of your parents, friends, colleagues, partner. Take your time to recall these past memories to your consciousness. Again, these will often diminish in power after they have been allowed an airing.

Your mental images: Close your eyes and allow yourself to experience your uncomfortable feelings. Let an image come — in as much detail as possible — and look at it. How did you create it? What does it do to you physically and emotionally? Write this picture down in words as clearly as you can. Now allow another image to form. This time picture shows how you would feel and react if you responded in a more positive way to that situation.

Your true wants and needs: Examine exactly what you desire. Write down 'I want' statements. Focus on these and how you may be negatively programming yourself *not* to achieve these desires. Write down the opposite of what you want or need in a second column. Be with that and see how you feel. Does it perhaps feel more comfortable?

How you can change: Now you can begin to affirm what you truly want. Write out your own affirmations in a positive way. Really feel and believe in these positive statements you are making. As you write, visualize these actually happening to you. If you want to change your job, write 'I *have* a new job' and picture yourself in a new working environment, with new faces, doing whatever job it is you wish to do. Reinforce your affirmations. Read them. Say them. Repeat them. Believe in them — and they'll be!

Happiness is a state of mind for which you, and you alone, are responsible. You cannot always be totally happy, but by developing unconditional acceptance, love, and forgiveness, an inner peace can be achieved in which you are *always* satisfied. Loving more, both ourselves and others, is imperative. The more love you both give and receive, the more you are able to release your full potential and open up to this state of inner peace.

Acceptance of yourself and others, compassion and genuine concern is part of the process of opening your heart. Learn to love and forgive more, and let go of those ill feelings and resentments. Appreciating your life and living fully in the pesent enhances awareness and is more likely to produce the optimum conditions for physical well-being. Opening your heart is not only an important aspect in regard to developing spiritual awareness, but also allows us to touch, and release, the energy we have centred at our heart level. Loving unconditionally, creating feelings of love, warmth and compassion for, not only our 'loved ones', but towards those as well for whom we have felt hurt or been wronged by, is not an overnight process and will probably come and go, but once you have embarked on the right path the transformation will occur without conscious effort on your part.

When you become relaxed and aware you are experiencing your own centre of calm and peace. When you are centred, you can observe with clarity your own actions, words, thoughts, deeds, feelings and behaviour, without judgement, guilt, anger or pain. Connecting with this centre (which occurs with any state of deep relaxation or meditation) enables you to feel less vulnerable; you are seeing yourself as detached from that which threatens you. Becoming centred involves quieting the mind, such as in meditation. When you still your mind and slow down the continual activity, you will become more controlled, less judgemental, less analytical.

Becoming centred takes time, so expect at first to notice only slight changes. You may find you are only centred at times when things are going well for you, when you are in a happy, joyous mood, but as soon as something occurs to disrupt that peaceful pattern — crash! down you go. Don't allow this to undermine your previous efforts. Expect this to happen at the beginning and simply recognize it when it comes, and what it was that put you off-centre, and learn from it so that you will feel more in control when a similar incident occurs. Gradually you will find this happens less and less: you will be steadily balanced to deal with all — good and bad — that comes to you.

Try these tow exercises. The first will help you to centre and to open your heart, and the second will bring you in touch with the pain and hurt from your past that can now, in the present, be forgiven.

Exercise 1.
Sitting in a comfortable position, close your eyes and focus for a few minutes on your breathing; letting all outside distractions fade away. Now bring your attention to your chest region and to the area of the heart. Bring to mind those experiences which have created great joy and love in your heart. Focus on these feelings as you begin to re-create them. Holding this awareness, allow and accept whatever comes up. If you begin to feel uneasy, just go back to concentrating on your breathing until the feeling has subsided and you feel calm again. Let the feeling of energy that has been created fill your heart, and as this grows more and more powerful, imagine your heart is opening up like the petals on a flower: see each petal slowly unfold as this love flows out of your heart. Now send those waves of love out to to a person whom you feel is in need of your love, whether this is someone with whom you already have a close bond or a person towards whom you have been feeling very negative.

Exercise 2.
You can either follow on from Exercise 1 or use this exercise on its own. After bringing your mind and body to a state of stillness, imagine you are out in the blue sky and visualize writing the word 'forgiveness'. Make the letters as large as you possibly can so that the whole sky is filled with 'forgiveness'. As you focus on this word, ask yourself who or what you need to forgive. Do not rush or force images or words to come, just be with the feeling and allow whatever occurs to happen as it pleases. Ask for your whole being to be filled with understanding and forgiveness so that you can release the resentment you are holding.

As you forgive the person(s) or situations that need forgiving, see the word 'forgiveness' slowly fading away as it becomes a part of *you* and no longer an outside entity.

We all, as humans, emit waves of energy that interrelate with other energy forms such as X-rays, light waves, radio waves, forces of gravity, etc. This energy can expand and contract according to our own emotional feelings. For instance, each time you act from your heart level, sending out love, compassion, forgiveness and other spiritual qualities, your energy waves increase. If you are filled with fear, anger, or other negative emotions, your energy flow is limited. Likewise, worrying over problems blocks the energy flow's smooth passage. This energy (known as *chi* to the Chinese, *ki* to the Japanese, *mana* to the Polynesians, *prana* to the Hindus, and *orenda* to the American Indians) is the concept the Chinese healing art of acupunture works on: disease setting into the area of the body where this energy has become blocked and unable to flow. This flow of inward and outward energy is known to the Chinese as yin and yang: yin being the female, receptive force and yang the male, aggressive force. As in breathing where we need to inhale and exhale, we need a balance of yin and yang to ensure a continual flow of this life force.

This energy is also healing energy and is most detectable in the hands and fingertips. You can experience this energy quite easily, as I will show you. Settle yourself in a comfortable position with your feet placed firmly on the ground, and with your eyes closed. Take several deep breaths and let your whole body relax. Then, when you are ready, raise your hands with the palms facing each other about twelve inches apart. Start to bring your palms together slowly until they are almost touching. Now draw away again. Notice what sensations you feel, either in your palms and/or fingertips. Is there heat? cold? tingling? Continue with this steady rhythm of drawing your hands together, then apart, decreasing in distance each time. Do you experience any differences between sensations when you change distances? Stay with this for a minute or two, then stop and rub your hands briskly together and go over the same process again. Note your experience this time and any changes in energy. Finally, repeat the process, this time while creating a mental image of love. Create this wonderful glowing experience in whatever way you choose. How has the energy in your hands changed? Your hands may now feel like magnets being drawn together, the energy much stronger and warmer.

That is an exercise I use with participants in my workshops and there is always an exclamation of surprise from those present never before having tapped into this subtle energy form. Practise with the exercise until you become fully in accordance with your own healing energy, for this is a primer to developing your healing power to help others.

I believe that we all have the ability to heal. But it is like playing a piano: anyone can learn, but some have greater gifts. That is not, however, to say that with practise we cannot develop our healing ability further. People are doing it more than they think, though. Sometimes it can come in the form of a kind word or deed, occurring in another's life just at the right moment when they are most receptive. Healing is really about caring, concern, love, and a willingness to be of service to others. Healing is the most simple thing in the world and I don't believe you have to have a degree in medical science or a vast knowledge of Gray's Anatomy to be an effective healer. I don't, and I think the results I have achieved up to now speak for themselves. I work entirely from intuition; channeling unconditional universal love — God — the great spirit, whatever. I believe I start a ball rolling, providing the impetus or push, but healing is only a small part of the process. The most important thing is to reach out to someone and touch them spiritually.

Healing is largely the reaction and interaction between two people when they come together: how these two relate, intellectually and emotionally; how their individual energies interrelate with each other, and the spark that is ignited, forming the starting point for healing to take place. This need not pertain to hands-on healing. We are all healers in the sense that we can, and do, affect others constantly with whatever kind of energy we are transmitting at that particular time, and we ourselves are affected likewise. We have all at one time or another, had the experience of being enlivened and inspired in a particular person's presence, and of feeling quite drained and sombre after having been in the company of another. We may also provide the catalyst — or have the same provided for us — that is needed by another to initiate their self-healing process. This could be sparked off by something as simple as taking the time to listen to them with total attention and share their anxieties (or having someone respond to you in the same way: allowing you a safe space to talk freely without judgement or criticism). Or by recommending a book, therapist, growth course. Or it could even be a small, but meaningful, gesture such as a pat on the arm, a kiss on the cheek, an affectionate hug, or a sympathetic smile. Whatever the act may be, somewhere inside the other person this gesture takes on the crucial implication of providing the spiritual turning point needed to move forward.

Touch is an important aspect in healing. I mentioned earlier how a number of my patients will start to cry during their healing session after I have placed my hands on their shoulders to begin. I feel this touch releases whatever pain they may have suppressed inside, perhaps for many years. Psychotherapist and cancer counsellor Stephanie Matthews Simonton relates in her book *The Healing Family* her experience of sitting with patients and gently stroking or holding their hands, without speaking, and having them break down in tears. She has found on many occasions this simple, yet caring, act seems to burst the dam and allows the patient relief from their pent-up feelings.

Research and experience indicate the importance of hugging and touching. It is regarded by therapists and counsellors in the mental health field as an intense way to communicate physically with another. Studies have also revealed that if a small premature baby is touched and cuddled daily he has far fewer apneic (non-breathing) periods and gains weight far quicker than those babies who have received little or no physical contact.

In early 1986 a major scientific study was initiated at the Hammersmith Hospital, London, neonatal intensive care unit. The study — the first of its kind — is based on an ancient technique discovered centuries ago by South American natives, who found that a fragile baby cuddled between its mother's breasts and against her heart, could gain a great deal of much needed warmth and security. Hammersmith Hospital is now trying the treatment, and preliminary findings are reported to be encouraging. Specialists who brought the technique to London from Bogota, Columbia, believe that having the mother hold their baby to their heart, for hours at a time, to ease them through the shock and stress in the early weeks following premature birth, can provide a psychological booster to the infant's growth and sense of security.

Right from birth there is an imperative need within all of us to be tenderly loved and cared for. Failure to receive adequate nurturing in the formative years can lead to both emotional and physical difficulties later in life. Dr Maurice J. Rosenthal stated in 1952 in an article produced in *Paediatrics*, entitled 'Psychosomatic Study of Infantile Eczema', that his hypothesis that eczema 'arises in certain predisposed infants because they fail to obtain from their mother adequate physical soothing contact, caressing and cuddling' was confirmed in a study of 25 mothers with children under the age of two suffering from eczema. The majority of these infants had mothers who had failed to give them a sufficient amount of skin-to-skin contact.

The mother's cuddling of a child plays a large and vital role in its subsequent sexual development: children who have been infrequently held and cuddled will suffer in adolescence and adulthood from an affect-hunger for such attention. It was also stated by psychiatrist Anna

Freud that 'being stroked, cuddled and soothed by touch . . . helps to build up a healthy body image and body ego.' Those who are parents will know that a small child who is upset or frightened can be soothed and made to feel secure again by being held in the arms of the mother or father. Putting your arms around another is a way of expressing love, without need of words. Rhythmic rocking of a person while holding them is an added means of comfort. This probably goes back to the period before birth when the baby is surrounded by fluid in the mother's womb and is rocked by the normal motions of her body.

Kathleen Keating, a mental health counsellor and consultant in California, and conductor of seminars and workshops across the United States on health, well-being and stress management, calls hugging 'a mutually healing process . . . you are open to the child within you who needs love, safety, support, caring and play, and you are reaching out to the same needs in the other.'

We have seen from experiments that touch not only induces physiological changes (as in the 'therapeutic touch' of former nursing professor, Dolores Krieger), but it also improves our sense of self-worth ('He actually hugged *me*! I *must* be okay after all!'), helps us to feel good about ourselves and others, and diminishes our sense of loneliness and isolation. If you are a person who does not find it easy to spontaneously hug or express affection in a touching way, there is an exercise you may care to try to help you understand where your present attitudes stem from, and how and what you learnt about closeness and bodily contact while growing up.

Settle yourself in a comfortable position in a place away from noise and distraction. With your eyes closed, focus on breathing from your abdomen (this can be done by placing your hands on your stomach. Breathe in deeply so that your abdomen rises as you inhale and falls as you exhale). Gradually, when you are ready, bring into your mind the image of a television screen. Then, as if you were watching a video re-run of your life, re-trace your life back to your earliest visual memories of touching. Re-live that experience as if it were happening again right now in the present. Let all visions — and conversations, if any — float onto and off your mental television screen of their own accord, continuing until you feel ready to switch off your video. Take a few deep breaths, let the images gently and slowly fade away, and bring yourself back to the room and open your eyes.

At this point it may be useful to have a pen and paper ready so that you can note your immediate feelings. What insights came from what you had seen and/or heard? What did you recall experiencing in relation to hugging as a child? To whom did these images relate; was there a special significance? Are you satisfied with what you were taught about touching while growing up? If not, can you envisage changing to *new* attitudes?

It is not only the caressing and caring expressed towards, and received from, other human beings that is beneficial to our lives. Pets, too, have a strong impact on our emotional states.

Psychiatrist Dr Aaron Katcher of the University of Pennsylvania, and one of the leading researchers of the human-animal bond, in studying the effects stroking and patting had on lowering both the animal and human's blood pressure, found that both man and beast experience a significantly lower blood pressure during the process. Following a group of 92 coronary patients between 1975 and 1977, one year after discharge from hospital only 3 of the 53 pet owners had died; compared with 11 of the 39 without pets. The difference could not have been due to the exercising that dogs require, found Katcher, since there were no deaths either among the 10 patients who owned pets *other* than dogs. However, it appears that this beneficial relaxation response is only produced with an animal to whom one is already bonded. Dr Katcher believes that stroking and talking to a pet cat or dog acts on stimulating the production of endorphins — the brain's own natural pain-killers and relaxation chemicals.

It is also established that passive contemplation of animal life is a plus to human health. In 1984 a study was carried out in Philadelphia on patients all about to submit to dental surgery. They were split into three groups: one group being hypnotized, another was asked to sit and look at fish swimming around in an aquarium, and the third group sat and read. It was found that viewing the fish was as effective as being hypnotized, and both these groups experienced the least anxiety, reducing both blood pressure and heart rates. The effect was strong enough to enable patients to continue in the relaxed state during surgery itself by closing their eyes and visualizing the aquarium again.

Pets also serve a purpose in directing attention away from oneself. It has been found that owning a pet generally fulfils seven distinct functions for their owners: (1) companionship, (2) something to care for, (3) something to touch and fondle, (4) something to keep one busy, (5) a focus of attention, (6) exercise, and (7) safety.

Dr Robert Miller, a Californian vet, states: 'I have learned that there is no such thing as a "pet". The companion animals that we designate as pets — whether they be dogs, or cats, or cage birds — fill very specific roles in their owners' lives. They may be an expression of our alter ego. They may serve as totems — as symbols of something that we are or wish to be — as trappings. They serve in role playing. And, above all, they serve as surrogates — surrogate friends, children, mates, parents, servants, and even masters.'

In a BBC-1 documentary shown in 1986 on the work of the Blue Cross Animal Hospital in London, an elderly lady with a shopping trolley containing four Pekinese dogs was asked by the interviewer why she had four, and weren't they a lot to look after. Her vehement reply was that they were 'her life'. She explained that she had rescued them when she heard they were to be put down by a neighbour who was moving abroad and could not take them with her. Looking after them had given her, she said, something to get up for each day, something to care for. 'I saved their life', she went on, 'and they saved mine.'

You cannot be of service to others in using your ability to heal if you feel restricted in your closeness to another human body, and in placing your hands upon them. One way to overcome this is through massage. This healing, relaxing art is an ideal way to connect us with another human being, in both giving and receiving, to induce calm and relaxation. It is a simple, easily learnt technique that goes back to the days of the ancient Greeks and Romans; that brings us into skin-to-skin contact and to tenderly care for and treat another with our hands, to alleviate tensions where the muscles have contracted (particularly in the neck and shoulders), and encourage lymphatic drainage. Massage can also act as a natural painkiller. Conducted in a comfortable and harmonious atmosphere where both partners feel at ease, massage provides an excellent basis for experience in moving your hands to the area you intuitively sense tightness or a change in skin temperature, muscle tension etc. Imparting with your hands a gentle, soft and caring touch and allowing yourself to go with the rhythm of the massage strokes (the long stroking movement of *effleurage*, the rhythmic lifting and rolling of *petrissage*, the rapid firm movement of *friction*, the chopping motion of *tapotment*), you will gradually let go of any inhibitions you may have held at the outset, and at the same time heighten your sensitivity to another's energy. Initially, if you have never given a massage before, it might be better to practise on someone you know well and feel at ease with, such as your partner or a close friend or relative: this will allow you both to feel comfortable and secure and obtain feedback on techniques of giving from the receiver.

Illness is often an opportunity for growth, and it very often comes about that those who have been through potentially life-threatening illness, emerge with a deeper love, compassion and empathy, for while we can all feel concern and sympathy for those in crisis, we can only *truly empathize* and *feel the experience* when we have surmounted our own similar dark days. For those who have fought and won their battle with serious illness, we commonly hear how coping through those long, harrowing days have brought about a change in personality. Take, for example, U.S. President Franklin D. Roosevelt. An acute appendicitis in 1914 was followed seven years later by polio, which left him wheelchair-bound for the rest of his life. With the urging of his wife Eleanor he resumed his successful political career and became a different person. To quote his wife: 'Franklin's illness proved a blessing in disguise, for it gave him strength and courage which he had not had before,' and one of his colleagues later commented that Roosevelt had undergone 'a spiritual transformation during the years of his illness. The man emerged completely warm-hearted with humility of spirit and a deeper philosophy, having purged the slightly arrogant attitude he had displayed before.'

Another example is that related by Rachael Clyne in her book *Coping With Cancer*, which tells of her personal experiences when her husband was diagnosed with testicular cancer in 1982. His recovery programme (combined with surgery, chemotherapy, and 'his own total commitment to get better'), she says, was 'an opportunity to change the quality of his life to a happier and more fulfilled expression.' For him, cancer was a 'transformative experience' during which he was 'able to come to terms with lifelong feelings of resentment and self-hatred . . . he developed a new faith and confidence.' And there are many, many others who have overcome all the odds stacked against them to emerge with a new-found zest for living and a profound change in personality.

While I have concentrated so far throughout on my work as a healer in helping people to become well and improve their quality of life, my work is equally to help someone to die in peace, without pain or suffering. I have come to the conclusion that we all have an allotted time span for being on this earth, and that everything that happens to us in life is for our own spiritual growth and evolution. Things happen, in other words, for a purpose and not just by chance. When our allotted time span is up, there comes another time of growth: of our being accepting and ready for our own death; which is described by Ian Gawler — an Australian vetinerary surgeon and author of *You Can Conquer Cancer*, who was expected to live no longer than a few weeks when secondary cancer developed in 1976, and more than eleven years later is still alive and well — as being like 'slipping off an old well-worn raincoat after a hard day's work, leaving the body and entering the warmth and security of a glowing home.'

My first experience in healing came shortly after I had decided to put my foot down and stop doing experiments influencing infra-red beams and the like, in order to concentrate on work of a more worthwhile and positive nature. A man arrived at my home one day and introduced himself as an Italian doctor, who had heard of the cancer cell experiments I had done in America, and asked would I be prepared to go and see his mother who was in a hospital in England very ill with cancer. It wasn't the kind of thing I had ever done before and I was certainly rather hesitant about doing it, but it is very hard to say no when you have someone standing there pleading with you. So I went along to the hospital, not knowing whether I could help or not, but prepared to do whatever I could. I can still recall the terrific shock it gave me to see someone quite so ill as this woman was. However, I put my hands on her and began to work in the same way as I had done with the cancer cells in the flask. Within a few hours — to my amazement — this woman was walking around a little, had eaten the first solid meal she had taken in weeks, and generally looked much brighter than before I had given her healing. I was naturally delighted; however, my feeling of elation was not to last for long, when I discoveed the next morning that she had, in fact, died during the night. I felt I had failed; my sense of sadness and disappointment was indescribable: I had *so* wanted it to work. It was only later, with much hindsight and greater experience, that I realized that in many ways the healing *hadn't* been a failure: it had succeeded in the fact that the woman had died peacefully and comfortably, without feeling terribly sick or in pain.

Another experience of this kind which had a strong effect on me, occurred a few years ago while I was on a lecture tour in the United States. A little boy aged seven was brought to me, suffering from a rare disease, for healing. Looking at him as he sat slumped and strapped into a wheelchair, I wondered if there was anything left I could do: already well over $1½ million had been paid out in medical insurance to keep him alive. I began to give him healing, and as I did so I experienced two conflicting sensations, something which I had never before encountered. While I sense on the one hand that the healing *had* worked, I also strangely felt that in some way it hadn't, or rather, that there was nothing I could do for the boy. I was to find the answer to this intriguing puzzle several months later. Back in England a letter arrived one morning from the mother of this small boy, in which she said, 'I just wanted to thank you for the healing you gave my son. It was one hundred-per-cent successful. Exactly one week to the hour my son died, at peace and free from pain for the first time in his life. Thank you.' That experience has remained strongly in my mind and I think it is a good example of how healing can work in not only helping the sick and afflicted to get well, but also in releasing those for whom the hour has dawned to 'slip off their well-worn raincoat.'

We must also bear in mind that for those who have given up, feel they have nothing more to live for, and have made up their minds they no longer want to go on, we can only acquiesce to their personal wish (and make their passing as comfortable and as pain-free as possible), or attempt a healing of the spirit: the former perhaps being the most appropriate in cases of advanced terminal illness where the person has already come to terms with dying and is ready to be released.

Rosemary and Victor Zorza's daughter Jane was just 25 when she learned she had cancer of the skin and stomach (with secondaries in the lymph glands). When she died five months later, her death was not a giving in, but a *triumph* over cancer in another way: a victory against pain and fear. Spending her last weeks in a hospice, she faced death with ease and tranquillity, and kept free from pain with medication, 'she met her end surrounded by love, with all emotional debts paid and the pattern of her life complete,' write the Zorzas (*A Way To Die: Living To The End*). 'She was ready for what she knew must come, accepting it with a serenity that belied her early fears.'

Death of the spirit, a sense of there being nothing left to live for, is easily seen in the case of Labour politician Herbert Morrison. Totally blind in his right eye practically from birth, he overcame this handicap to become one of the leading figures in shaping the Labour Party policies of the 30's and 40's. He was appointed President of the Board of Film Censors in 1960, and although he gave up his Labour Party work in 1962 (at the age of 74), he still continued to devote time to the House of Lords; and when in the autumn of 1964 he began to lose the sight in his good left eye through a progressive untreatable disease of the retina, stoically he refused to allow this to depress him, and would have a colleague rehearse his speeches aloud to him so that he could speak from memory. Shortly before Christmas 1964 there came, what was to him, an even bigger blow when he was informed by The Kinematograph Manufacturers' Association that his contract would not be renewed. Morrison took the news badly and from then on his spirits noticeably sagged. In early February the following year he was admitted to hospital suffering from inflammation of the large intestine — a painful, but treatable, condition. At first he seemed to be rallying, but when his personal physician informed him that he would soon be well enough to leave, Morrison is said to have responded, 'What have I got to recover for? I cannot see. I've lost my job on the Film Censors' Board. There is nothing for me in politics . . .' He died on 6 March 1965. The cause of death was attributed to a cerebral haemorrhage; in a later interview his doctor stated: 'If you ask me what he died of, I don't know. He just died because he saw no further point in living.'

We will all die one day. It is as much a fact of life as is our birth and years in between. Developing a positive approach to death is as important as adopting a positive approach to life: they complement each other. While facing up to the prospect of death will never be easy, it can be made easier by facing our feelings openly and honestly; by releasing them, and by being able to express them for as long as we may need. Talking with others about death and dying leads to a 'letting go': a release of the associated fear-based problems such as the fear of leaving all that is known, the fear of the actual process of dying itself, and the fear of entering the realms of the unknown. Such shared communication in discussing both the practical and spiritual aspects leads to increased bonding and allows an outlet for suppressed fears, depression, anger and other emotions.

In all Eastern literature, and that of the Tibetan Buddhists in particular, we find the utmost importance given to dying, with the moment of death looked upon as spiritual liberation; the idea being to remain conscious and alert. *The Tibetan Book of the Dead* speaks of *bardos* (the periods before and after death) offering challenges to the soul on the path to enlightenment. When these are faced with ease and calm, then all fears are just mere projections of one's own mind. The dying person is reminded not to become entangled in these illusions, but to go on practising the art of living even while they are dying. In a talk given at the San Francisco Gestalt Institute some years ago, Ram Dass (former professor of psychology at Harvard University, spiritual teacher and author), reflecting on dying, agreed with this philosophy saying, 'The game is to stay fully conscious at the moment of death — so that, as you're dying, as the body goes, you're right here, and it's just a continuum of consciousness even though the body falls off. Otherwise you can get caught in the pain or the melodrama of the fear of ceasing to be who you thought you were.'

Aldous Huxley, author of *Brave New World*, *Island* and *Eyeless in Gaza*, amongst others, watched his first wife Maria die of cancer in 1955. In an account written after her death, he tells of his feelings and experiences, and relates how a psychotherapist friend would come in, in the weeks beforehand, and put her into hypnosis; giving her suggestions to ease the nausea, which Huxley himself would then follow up using similar suggestions for muscular relaxation, '. . . these were followed by a much longer series of suggestions addressed to the deeper levels of the mind. I would remind her of the desert she had loved so much, of the vast crystalline silence of the overarching sky, of the snow-covered mountains; the desert sky . . . to think of it as the bluelight of Peace . . ..I would urge her to advance into those lights, to open herself to joy, peace, love and being, and to become one with them. I kept on repeating this, urging her to go deeper and deeper into the light.' In the last hour or so of her life, Huxley remained with her, telling her still 'to let go, to forget the body, to leave it lying here like a bundle of old clothes and to allow herself to be carried into the heart of the rosy light of love.' Shortly before 6 a.m. on 12 February 1955, Maria Huxley ceased breathing, without any struggle. Aldous Huxley himself died with similar ease eight years later (also of cancer), with his second wife Laura urging him to ' "go forward into the light. It is easy and you are doing this beautifully and consciously, in full awareness, darling, you are going toward the light." I repeated these or similar words for the last three or four hours. The ceasing of life was not a drama at all, but like a piece of music just finishing, so gently in a sempre piú piano, dolecemente . . . and at five-twenty the breathing stopped.'

Most of us when faced with serious illness and death will go through stages of anger, denial, bargaining, depression and finally, acceptance. These five stages are commonplace in all serious illness as well as following bereavement, or indeed, a loss of any kind, and was first defined by psychiatrist and expert in the bereavement and grief field, Elisabeth Kübler-Ross. A typical reaction is 'Why me?', wondering what you have done to deserve it, and a feeling that it is unfair. Denial is a protection, a refusing to accept that one has anything wrong, or that a loved one has died. While this may provide protection, for a while, it also delays plans and matters of importance that may have to be done and made for the future. Bargaining can take various forms: mental pacts with God ('If you just let me get well and not die, I promise I'll go to church ever week.') or in other ways in which a promise is given in exchange for delaying death.

Depression is paramount in most illness, from a mild dose of 'flu to a potentially life-threatening disease, and will be experienced by both the patient and their family, friends and loved ones. The love and comfort that all involved can provided for each other during these times is of the greatest help and support. Finally, when one accepts that they have an illness, yet can still achieve the maximum quality of each day, recognizing and accepting that some days will be better than others, an easing of much of the stress and depression will result.

I'd like you, at this point, to stop reading for a while and focus your thoughts on your own personal awareness of death. Retrace events back through your life where you have encountered a loss — for many the first experience of a death may well be that of a much loved pet — can you recall how you felt at the time, what your emotions and reactions were, and what you were told by your father and mother about the death? Place yourself back in those situations again. How were others (parents, siblings, relatives, friends) acting at this time? Observe your thoughts and feelings. Go through and recollect the events and actions surrounding all the significant bereavements you have had in your life. Now, relate this to your own being, and your own death. When did you first have any notion that you, too, would one day die? How did you feel when that realization first came to you? Has that changed — how do you view your own death now? What kind of death do you visualize for youself?

We often refer to those who live dangerous or seem to actively court an early demise, as having a 'death wish'; and if we adhere to the idea of energy following thought, then this may well result, that the way you wish to end your life, if repeatedly played out (i.e. if you are a fast, reckless driver, you may well end your life in a fatal car accident; if you are 'sure' your days will end in extreme pain and fear, they probably will) will form your own personal blueprint. What you believe and affirm will surely come to pass. You *can* change that blueprint. Your diary or journal can be useful here in recording your fears, mental images and expectations of death and dying, and recognizing how perhaps your preconceived impression of death is being given power in your day-to-day living.

Some might also view it as a kind of 'death wish' when those who have been making reasonable progress following a serious illness, give up in the way of slipping into a state of complacency. Suddenly all the effort they have been putting into their health recovery programme (perhaps relating to diet, meditation, positive attitude, relaxation, 'hope for the future', etc.) stops. This can occur for a number of reasons: feeling so much better, that they are now 'over the worst', they begin to fall back into their old ways and habits (for many, probably the very things that helped bring about their illness in the first place); an event — bereavement, job loss, marital discord — occurs which initiates a feeling of 'I've put *all this effort* into getting well only for *this* to happen . . .' Suddenly the scales tip heavily to one side and the sense of 'no hope' that they may have had at the outset of the illness returns; or they may experience a recurrence of the illness, or another may appear. Again: 'I've worked *so hard*, now I'm *just the same* once more.'

At this juncture it is well worth asking yourself the question 'Do I REALLY want to get well?' (Perhaps use the question to meditate upon and see what comes up, which might give you a clearer answer.) 'Of course I want to get well,' 'I'd like to feel better but I feel so despondent now I've lost my job/husband/wife . . .', 'Now I'm feeling so fit and busy getting on with my life, I simply don't have the time to prepare a special diet/meditate/relax more etc.' might be some of the answers. But there is one very simple overriding fact: if you value your health then you'll start being a little kinder to yourself. That means stopping rushing around doing a dozen things at once just because you feel much better — because you can guarantee that before long you'll undo all the previous good you have put into getting better. Talk over problems, don't bottle them up inside. I mentioned earlier in this chapter how through centring yourself you can feel more in control and remain perfectly balanced to deal with life events and situations as and when they arise. Remember that your illness was probably a major turning point in your life, and while it may be easy to slip back into your old patterns of actions and thoughts, would it really, truly and honestly, be worth it in terms of quality of life?

Penny Brohn, co-founder of the Bristol Cancer Help Centre, successfully fought breast cancer when it was first detected in 1979. Four years later, when a second lump was found in the same breast, she fought and won again. This time, however, she questioned *why* it had happened to her a second time — what was this second tumour trying to tell her. She realized that she had allowed herself to become a 'crazy workaholic . . .. There was hardly a moment of my time used to replenish myself.' Things such as diet, vitamins and meditation had become items hastily, and haphazardly, incorporated into a busy day. But probably the most crucial realization to Penny the second time around, was that the healing she required was a long-term *process* and not a singular event. Looking back now she can say: 'Through knowing myself and accepting myself a little better I find it easier to live for now. To be fully in this moment. (Before) I didn't want to live for the present because it was always tangled up with my past failures. The healing that I know has taken place lies in this: that the present is all right with me.' (From *Gentle Giants*, Century, 1987).

Be a little kinder to yourself. Nurture and be tender to that little child that is still within you. However 'old' we may be in terms of physical years, the small child we once were still remains somewhere locked away inside. Take a few minutes to go back to those long hazy days of your childhood. Look at yourself as you were at the age of five or six, or younger perhaps, or older. Visualize yourself exactly as you remember looking and acting at that age. Now bring to mind a time when you were at that age where you felt particularly upset and sad over something, and how you were comforted and made to feel happy and secure again. Gradually come back to the present to whatever age you are now, and play the loving parent to that small child within you. Offer that child words of comfort and support. Tell the child that things *will* be better; perhaps offer it a token to 'take the pain away' (what can you recall being given as a child? An ice-cream? A toy? How about offering yourself a nice cup of tea? Or that new record you've been promising yourself?). If it's easier, take a cushion and use that to represent your inner child. Hold it, stroke it, rock it, talk lovingly to it; offer it love, warmth and comfort.

A recurrent theme throughout most of Aldous Huxley's life was that 'One never loves enough'. In a lecture shortly before he died, he said, 'It is a little embarrassing that, after forty-five years of research and study, the best advice I can give to people is to be a little kinder to each other.'

That is the best advice I, too, could probably give — with an addendum:

Be a little kinder to each other — and to yourself.

Matthew Manning has a range of video and audio tapes available. Information about these can be obtained from:

The Matthew Manning Centre
39 Abbeygate Street, Bury St Edmunds
Suffolk IP33 1LW

Telephone: (0284) 69502

Further reading

Amodeo, John and Kris, *Being Intimate: A Guide to Successful Relationships* (Arkana, 1986).

Benson, Herbert, MD, *The Relaxation Response* (Fount Paperbacks, 1984).

——, *Beyond the Relaxation Response* (Fount Paperbacks, 1985).

Blakeslee, Thomas R., *The Right Brain: A new understanding of the unconscious mind and its creative powers* (Macmillan, 1980).

Brohn, Penny, *Gentle Giants: The powerful story of one woman's unconventional struggle against breast cancer* (Century, 1986).

Clyne, Rachael, *Coping with Cancer* (Thorsons, 1986).

Cousins, Norman, *Anatomy of an Illness* (Bantam, 1987).

Edwards, Betty, *Drawing on the Right Side of the Brain* (Fontana, 1982).

Frankl, Viktor, *The Unheard Cry for Meaning* (Hodder and Stoughton, 1978).

Gawain, Shakti, *Living in the Light: A Guide to Personal and Planetary Transformation* (Whatever Publishing Inc., 1986).

Hodgkinson, Liz, *Smile Therapy: How Smiling and Laughter Can Change Your Life* (Macdonald Optima, 1987).

Huxley, Laura Archer, *This Timeless Moment: A Personal View of Aldous Huxley* (Chatto & Windus, 1969).

Jampolsky, Gerald G., MD, *Low is Letting Go of Fear* (Bantam, 1981).

——, *Teach Only Love* (Bantam, 1983).

——. *Goodbye to Guilt* (Bantam, 1985).

Keating, Kathleen, *The Little Book of Hugs* (Angus & Robertson, 1986).

Krieger, Dolores, Ph.D., *The Therapeutic Touch* (Prentice-Hall Inc., 1979).

Levine, Stephen, *Who Dies?* (Anchor Doubleday, 1982).

Muller, Robert, *New Genesis: Shaping a Global Spirituality* (Doubleday, 1982).

——, *Decide to . . .* ('18 exhortations to inspire us and to waken us up') availabe from Acorn Publishing, March House, Ogbourne St George, Marlborough, Wiltshire SN8 1SU (£1.95 plus 50p p & p).

O'Neill, Cherry Boone, *Starving for Attention* (Dove Communications, 1982).

Pearsall, Dr Paul, *Super Immunity* (McGraw-Hill, 1987).

Powell, Ken, *Fight Stress and Win* (Thorsons, 1988).

Roet, Dr Brian, *Hypnosis: A Gateway to Better Health* (Weidenfeld & Nicolson, 1986).

——, *All in the Mind* (Macdonald Optima, 1987).

Roman, Sanaya, *Personal Power Through Awareness* (H.J. Kramer Inc., 1986).

Russell, Peter, *The Awakening Earth* (Arkana, 1988).

Shattock, E.H., *A Manual of Self-Healing* (Turnstone Press, 1982).

Siegel, Bernie S., MD *Love, Medicine and Miracles* (Rider, 1986).

Simonton, O. Carl, MD, *Getting Well Again* (Bantam, 1980).

Simonton, Stephanie Matthews, *The Healing Family* (Bantam, 1984).

Stanton, Dr H.E., *The Plus Factor: A Guide to Positive Living* (Macdonald Optima, 1988).

Zorza, Rosemary and Victor, *A Way to Die: Living to the End* (Andre Deutsch, 1980).

The following books contain substantial reference to Matthew Manning and his work

Harvey, David, *The Power to Heal* (Aquarian Press, 1983).

Inglis, Brian and West, Ruth, *The Alternative Health Guide* (Michael Joseph, 1983).

Lloyd Fraser, John, *The Medicine Men* (Thames/Methuen, 1981).

Manning, Matthew, *The Link* (Colin Smythe, 1974).

Van Straten, Michael, *The Complete Natural Health Consultant* (Ebury Press, 1987).

Index